Best Of

COZUMEL

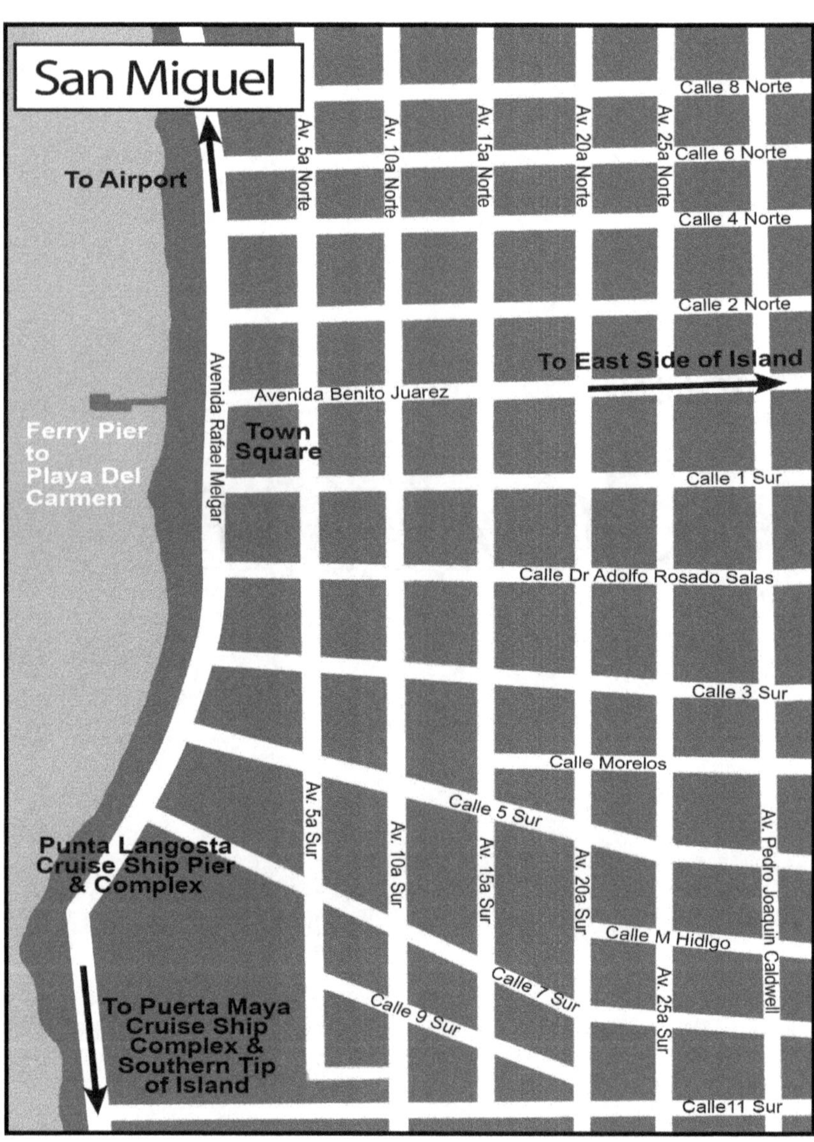

San Miguel
To Airport
Ferry Pier to Playa Del Carmen
Avenida Rafael Melgar
Av. 5a Norte
Av. 10a Norte
Av. 15a Norte
Av. 20a Norte
Av. 25a Norte
Calle 8 Norte
Calle 6 Norte
Calle 4 Norte
Calle 2 Norte
To East Side of Island
Avenida Benito Juarez
Town Square
Calle 1 Sur
Calle Dr Adolfo Rosado Salas
Calle 3 Sur
Calle Morelos
Punta Langosta Cruise Ship Pier & Complex
Av. 5a Sur
Calle 5 Sur
Av. 10a Sur
Av. 15a Sur
Av. 20a Sur
Av. Pedro Joaquin Caldwell
Calle M Hidlgo
To Puerta Maya Cruise Ship Complex & Southern Tip of Island
Calle 7 Sur
Calle 9 Sur
Av. 25a Sur
Calle11 Sur

Best Of
COZUMEL

A Traveler's Guide - To The Island's Best

JACKSON LINDSAY

LOCAL KNOWLEDGE TRAVEL GUIDES, LLC
MEQUON, WISCONSIN

PUBLISHED BY
LOCAL KNOWLEDGE TRAVEL GUIDES, LLC

Copyright © 2020 by Jackson Lindsay

Local Knowledge is a trademark of
Local Knowledge Travel Guides, LLC

Editor: Abby Lindsay
Photography: Jackson Lindsay

DEDICATION

Dedicated to my wife Sue, my kids Abby, Claire, and Willy,
and my mother, for their patience, heart, and understanding.

FOREWORD

Easily the most definitive guidebook available for the island of Cozumel, Local Knowledge Travel Guides/Best of Cozumel, contains an indispensable collection of uniquely categorized places to eat, drink, swim, explore, sun and shop.

Having been carefully assembled by its author, after 45 years of visiting the area, Local Knowledge/Cozumel also utilizes countless interviews with island divers, fishermen, vendors, artists, and expats to come up with the best spots. Know places that will fit your style for food and drink, romantic beaches, dive or fishing guides, live music, local art, quiet shopping spots, or top-notch silver your first day, without fumbling around with questionable suggestions. Too many first visits to unfamiliar ports can be met with disappointment and costly delays by simply not knowing where to go or wasting time with generic guidebooks. Local Knowledge is a compilation of favorite suggestions from people who have been there and done that. Carry it with you in your purse or bag, or on your preferred electronic device, read and enjoy, study it on the boat, plane or taxi, and have an excellent time.

Surprisingly, Cozumel is mostly undeveloped. Vast jungle, quiet ranches, miles of virgin coastline and beaches, scores of ancient Mayan ruins remain unpreserved and hidden deep in the jungles. You would never know this if your only introduction to the island were its major town San Miguel (El Cedral is the second town, we will discuss later), the 6 some odd miles which make up the northern hotel district, the ferry pier and the three cruise ship terminals south of town. Other than this busy stretch, the visitor to Cozumel can expect a lot of peace and quiet, remarkable dining with excellent local fare, to tastes representing nearly all corners of the world, and some of the world's finest diving in the heart of the Mesoamerican Reef, the second-largest barrier reef in the world.

Located in the Caribbean Sea about 12 miles east of Playa Del Carmen and the Yucatan mainland, the island itself is roughly 30 miles long by 10 miles wide at the widest point. While only a few miles and crystal-clear water separate the two, any similarity aside from proximity ends there. Cozumel is a humble community that has been welcoming visitors with gracious and open arms long before any resort existed on the mainland coast. Playa Del Carmen, Tulum, Puerto Morelos, and Cancun were destinations with little to no infrastructure whatsoever, but travelers were already somewhat well entrenched on Cozumel and Isla Mujeres. The "gringo trail", and its travelers seeking the mysteries of Mexico and Central America years ago, helped pave the way for today's generation of divers, backpackers, condo owners, expats, all-inclusive resorts, cruise ships and "fusion" restaurants that in many ways define this busy and well-appointed portion of Mexico's Caribbean coastline.

The author of these books, and his wife, were two of those early visitors who loved the remote simplicity and beauty of the Yucatan and the special warmth of its people. "Our only purpose in visiting Playa Del Carmen in those days was to catch the daily morning ferry to Cozumel. Playa had no restaurants or hotels; it was just a sleepy Puebla with a rickety ferry pier and empty beaches where we would camp and wait for any sight of the ferry in the morning", Jackson says. He offers a perspective on the area which few have and lays it out for you in the pages ahead with a conversational style and a uniquely helpful format. Available exclusively from Local Knowledge Travel Guides.

Welcome to the island of Cozumel.

LOCAL KNOWLEDGE TRAVEL GUIDES

COZUMEL, MEXICO

HOW TO USE THIS BOOK

When visiting Cozumel, you are on Mexico's largest inhabited island, the country's largest Caribbean island, and the third-largest Mexican island overall. You will be on Mexico's second most eastern landmass and viewing a sunrise from the island's quiet and remote east side is something quite special. It is very close, but Isla Mujeres to the north by 50 miles or so, is the country's eastern-most landmass and the first to see the sunrise each morning. This is your guide to the magic of Cozumel.

For reference purposes and to help you easily find your way around, we will break the island up into 3 distinct areas. First, the only significant town on the island, San Miguel, where you will find the majority of restaurants, nightlife, and shopping. San Miguel is where the ferry comes across from the mainland port of Playa Del Carmen. It is where the island's international (but very quaint and tiny) airport is, and virtually all banks are in San Miguel. El Cedral is the only other town on the island, but it is very small and mostly residential, we will discuss it separately. The second area is the southwest coast which stretches from San Miguel town to the southern tip of the island. It is here and in San Miguel where you will find the island's 3 cruise ship piers. Once you pass the furthest south cruise ship pier (Puerta Maya), maybe 4 miles south of town, the island slows down to a true kick back and relax Caribbean pace. Finally, the third area is Cozumel's barren east coast where you will find a handful of fun and quiet little beach bars, one small and beautiful hotel, and miles of empty, picturesque stretches of beach. Everything closes down over here at about 6:00 p.m. and will begin to open again by 10:00 a.m. daily. There is no electricity, very spotty phone service and while the beaches are stunning, always beware of dangerous conditions, rip tides and undercurrents.

Reference Points:

1. **San Miguel Town:** The main dividing lines of San Miguel Town are either north or south of the pedestrian-only main Town Square directly across from the ferry port, or north and south of Avenue Benito Juarez in town, which is directly east of the pedestrian-only main square.
2. **The Malecon:** A common word in Spanish speaking countries for the waterfront walkway along the coast. Cozumel's is obvious and goes both north and south away from the main ferry pier.
3. **Avenida (avenue):** ALL roads running in a north-south direction parallel to the main waterfront road, Avenue Rafael Melgar. A few east-west roads are avenues as well (notably here Avenue Benito Juarez), but they are limited.
4. **Avenue norte (north avenue):** All avenues located north of the Town Square and north of Avenue Benito Juarez.
5. **Avenue sur (south avenue):** All avenues located south of the Town Square and south of Ave. Benito Juarez.
   **Avenues north or south begin one block east of the water. Avenida 5 is the first, then Avenida 10, followed by 15, and so on. They increase by 5 each block.
6. **Calle (street):** All streets running in an east-west direction.
7. **Calle Norte:** Streets that are located north of Town Square and Ave. Benito Juarez are even-numbered (i.e: Calle 2 norte, Calle 4 norte, etc.)
8. **Calle Sur:** All streets located south of the Town Square and Ave. Benito Juarez are odd-numbered (i.e. Calle 1 sur, Calle 3 sur, etc.)

   EXCEPTIONS: Common names are used for streets (Calles) or avenues (Avenidas) occasionally. Just keep track of the increase in the number in any direction, then use the included map and it's easy.

*Each spot cited in this book will be referenced by a location. We will refer to any location as near a cross street, or on a corner. For example, a particular market may be on the corner of Avenida 10 sur and Calle 5 Sur, or we may say, a restaurant is on Ave. 5 norte, between Calle 6 and 8 norte.

**Anything mentioned north of town is part of the 4 or so mile distance along the west coast between town and the Cozumel Country Club/Golf Course, where this road ends. This area encompasses mostly the one main road, several larger hotels, residences, and a lovely marina.

Right-of-Way When Driving: If in a vehicle, and you are moving in a north-south, or south-north direction, or parallel to the water, you theoretically have the right-of-way. If you are driving east-west or west-east, you need to stop at each intersection. It is advisable to exercise extreme caution when driving on the island, obey all signs, and do not take other drivers for granted. People take interesting liberties with driving regulations here. Be very careful. I will discuss bike lanes and cycling at a later point, and while there are visible bike lanes throughout the island, and in town, be cautious particularly in town as drivers do not always recognize these lanes or cyclists.

There are VERY busy sections, in particular along the main drag near the Playa Del Carmen ferry pier and south 3–4 miles toward the last cruise ship pier. Also, anywhere downtown in San Miguel can be busy with traffic and confusing to new drivers with mostly one-way streets. Once you are away from town and the cruise ship piers, driving on the island is quite easy with little traffic.

Remember, **pedestrians DO NOT have the right-of-way**, unless at an intersection regulated by local police. The only intersection regulated for pedestrians, on a regular basis, is the crossing of main street (Ave. Rafael Melgar) from the Playa Del Carmen ferry pier.

Street Signs and Stop Lights: Most street signs (names), are present at intersections, but usually not on posts like you may be used to. Street signs are more typically attached to the side of a building at the intersection. Stoplights will generally blink green before turning orange, be aware of this. ALWAYS look both ways when approaching any intersection with a vehicle or bicycle. The numerous one-way streets can be confusing, and vehicles parked at corners can easily obstruct your view of oncoming traffic.

(South of town to the southern tip of the island)

SOUTHWEST COAST

Reference Points:

> **Town of San Miguel**
> **Punta Langosta** – cruise ship pier located a few blocks south of the ferry pier to mainland
> **International Pier and Puerta Maya** – The 2 cruise ship piers 3–4 miles south of ferry pier

All locations mentioned in this section will be referenced by a certain distance from one of the three locations noted above.

The entire Southwest coast of which we speak stretches approximately 20 miles south of town. Once you reach 5 miles south of town or Puerta Maya cruise ship pier, development becomes more and more scarce. Also, just past Puerta Maya, the road splits heading south. The new road more specifically for cars goes straight, and the "old" road veers right, it is clearly marked.

EAST COAST ROAD

This road runs from Punta Sur Park on the Southern end to Mezcalito's on the Northern end, or about 11 miles. Nearly the entire east coast has 2 parallel roads, side by side. One is the old road and the other the new road. The old road, closest to the sea, is reserved for cyclists and we will discuss this later. The east coast of Cozumel is remote and beautiful with a handful of rustic beach bars, a stunning park (Punta Sur), a couple of lovely ranches, and miles of deserted beach. North of Mezcalito's there is a sand road that heads out to the northwest point of the island, Punta Molas. DO NOT take this road. You will get stuck and your insurance will be void. A handful of options are available for trips to Punta Molas, we will discuss them later in the book.

There are two routes you can choose from to reach the far east side of the island. Avenue Juarez in town becomes the straight road east across the middle of the island. The more scenic route beginning in town (Avenue Rafael Melgar), becomes the southwest coastal road as you drive south from town. Most opt to head south along this southwest coast where, after 20 miles or so, the road turns north again at Rastas Café and Punta Sur Park, and becomes the scenic east coast road. The first option mentioned Ave. Benito Juarez, turns into the transversal road and runs 11 miles or so to the east coast, and ends at the beach at Mezcalito's Restaurant.

One big hint! If you are returning to town on the road coming from the southern end, it gets VERY busy between 3:30 and 5:00 p.m.! Lots of people returning rental cars, getting back to their cruise ship, whatever. It can get very congested and is one lane, plan accordingly.

With the help of the enclosed maps, you ought to be well on your way to comfortably exploring the island and all that it has to offer.

Each establishment will be noted with a price marker:

Fairly expensive - $$$
Moderate - $$
Less expensive - $

Choose to be optimistic, it feels better."

Dali Lama

BEST DINING COZUMEL HAS TO OFFER

The dining options have exploded on this island in the last 10–15 years. Cajun food, French, Vegan, Italian, Sushi, English, Philippine, your choices are nearly endless on Cozumel. Of course, the local, Yucatecan and fresh seafood establishments, and many variations thereof, are still the prominent choice on the island. The fierce competition between restaurants takes its toll, as managers jump ship, wait staff, and kitchen help are difficult to procure and to keep, even owners move on at times. In other words, places can and do open and close here in the blink of an eye. Local Knowledge focuses on places that have shown some consistency and have established themselves on the island. Rarely will we jump on the hot new spot "bandwagon," and when we have it is amazing how many have closed!

We hesitate for the most part to include hours of operation or prices because high or low season may dictate changes. This may also affect the consistency of our information seasonally as some vendors will temporarily close, go on vacation or restrict hours during the low season. Thank you for your support, now go explore and you will discover the culinary beauty of Cozumel.

Restaurants NOT listed in order of significance.

" Life is either a daring adventure or nothing at all."

Helen Keller

BEST BREAKFASTS

La Choza Restaurant $

This long time favorite on the island has been in their new location for about 5 years now, right around the corner from their old spot. As legendary as any in Cozumel, La Choza is a popular breakfast spot though probably better known as a dinner destination for local families. Those who know Cozumel, locals, and tourists alike, come here time and time again. A simple destination with quite reasonable prices, La Choza is consistently wonderful, offering local and regional recipes for breakfast, lunch, and dinner. There is plenty of room here for large groups or an intimate corner for two.

Phone: 52-987-872-0958
(Calle 10 between AR Salas and 3 sur)

Casa Denis $

Long-standing for sure, Casa Denis is the oldest restaurant on the island. Casa Denis offers breakfast, lunch, and dinner. With delicious Yucatecan cuisine, this quiet location particularly early in the morning for breakfast makes for a nice spot to catch up on e-mails, enjoy a cup of coffee and fill up with a great Mexican breakfast. Sit outside along the pedestrian walk and watch the island wake up. Oddly, smoking is fine, but no cigars. There was a time when I would sit and read the paper here each morning when on the island, those days are gone!

Phone: 52-987-872-0067
(1/2 block up the pedestrian walkway off the southeast corner from the town square)

Restaurante Palmeras $$

Some may roll their eyes at the inclusion of this restaurant, but Palmeras is as iconic an island destination as any. You will see an equal clientele of old island families here as you will first-time visitors, Palmeras has something for everyone. Since 1976 this centrally located restaurant is impossible to miss and is maybe the most valuable real estate on the island. The same Cozumel family owns Pepe's down the street, which we will discuss later. Situated across the street from the Playa Del Carmen ferry pier, for close to 50 years Palmeras has been the first restaurant millions of visitors have seen upon arrival to the island. Due to its central location alone, nearly every visitor to Cozumel has stopped here at least once. While they do have decent Mexican breakfasts, they also serve any kind of omelet you could imagine. For the northern taste buds and the kids, the pancakes and waffles are great, if that is what you desire. Palmeras is fairly pricey and they provide breakfast lunch and dinner daily from 7:00 a.m.-10:00 p.m.

Phone: 52-987-872-0532

(Right across from the mainland ferry pier on Ave. Rafael Melgar)

Restaurante Costa Brava $

For a very local taste of breakfast, lunch, or dinner, this place is old-time Cozumel and as local as it gets. Good standard breakfasts with toast, eggs, potatoes, sausage, or bacon as well as great Mexican breakfast options. I have always loved stopping here for breakfast. Huevos Rancheros are delicious for breakfast, lunch or dinner, the seafood combination is simple but good with shrimp, octopus, lobster, conch, and fish (availability depends on the season). Also, try the fajitas or the shrimp flambe cooked right at your table. This is a very popular spot for local island families. They have gone through a few hiccups since the owner passed away a couple of years ago, but I still love Costa Brava.

(Calle 7 just east of the main drag, Ave. Rafael Melgar)

Museo De La Isla De Cozumel $$

The museum has been going through extensive remodeling for the past couple of years and its restaurant has been operating a few blocks south during this time. By March of 2020, the museum SHOULD be open again and the casual fun spot for breakfast on the 2nd-floor patio looking out over the water will be back with the same breathtaking views. The café offers a limited but excellent selection of Mexican breakfasts, along with a multitude of other egg dishes, bread selections, pastries, fresh fruit, and good coffees. The view is always sensational and is a beautiful way to begin the morning.

(On the waterfront between calle 4 norte and calle 6 norte)

La Candela $

La Candela is slowly establishing itself as a favorite breakfast stop on the island. Charming, a little away from the hustle of downtown, but only a 5-minute walk into a quiet neighborhood. The service is excellent, the décor pure Cozumel, and the food is always a treat, it is fresh, and arrives quickly. A variety of hot coffees and fresh juices, or try the fresh fruit, yogurt, and granola for a healthy start to the day. A selection of omelets and various egg dishes, fresh bread, chilaquiles with egg, cheese, or chicken, or my favorite the Mexican Sausage Burrito for a hearty breakfast. Divine in every way, La Candela is becoming a special island morning destination.

Phone: 52-987-878-4471

(SW corner of calle 6 & 5)

La Cozumeleña $

Another of the island's long-standing family-owned establishments which in my opinion has only one flaw. So, they have no outdoor seating, but everything else about La Cozumeleña is pure Cozumel vibe. Since 1962 they have grown into a remarkable but highly underrated island breakfast destination. Not only the restaurant but the complete bakery directly next door is nothing short of excellent. Anything from the bakery is available in the restaurant. Homemade bread, donuts, cheese bread, pies, pastries and so much more either for carry-out or for when you dine in. The breakfast crepes are excellent, from the caramel crepe to the cream cheese, or the sweet vegan crepe with strawberry, coconut oil, Nutella, avocado and cocoa. Fresh fruit, great omelets, ham and cheese croissant, or even pancakes. La Cozumeleña is one of the best on the island, enjoy.

Phone: 52-987-872-0189

(Corner of calle 3 & 2)

Zermatt Bakery $

This tiny European-like bakery has been in Cozumel for as long as I can remember. Everything is fresh and delicious daily like their excellent banana, orange and cinnamon

muffins, tasty fresh breads, and outstanding pastry sandwiches with ham, cheese, and other wonderful delights. Zermatt bakery is reminiscent of small bakeries in rural Austria, Switzerland or Germany. What it lacks in décor it makes up for with its mouthwatering tastes and sweet smells. A must! There are only 4–5 tables out front along the street on the small veranda, but the quiet street this bakery is on makes for a crowd-free light breakfast stop. The pigeons love this place as daily they are fed old bread out on the corner. Don't even think of smoking here, they make it very clear. It is usually open by 7:30 a.m. and closed by 2ish.

(SE corner of 5 avenue norte and calle 4 norte)

Rock 'N Java $$

So much is so very good here at this long-standing island institution. They for sure create a favorite Eggs Benedict, possibly anywhere, but that is a fraction of the excellence of Rock 'N Java. Along with the great view of the ocean, the bakery goods are delightful. Shakes, smoothies, and a local friend of mine swears by the Amaretto milkshake! They may lean a bit toward gringo tastes, but that is ok because you can still find excellent guacamole, empanadas, tacos, and quesadillas. The breakfast and brunch menus are extensive, so each individual in your group will find something. Dinner is served here as well, and you can choose to sit inside with AC or out on the deck. Really good Bloody Mary's!

Phone: 52-987-872-4405

(South of the Playa del Carmen ferry pier by 3–4 blocks right across from the Mega Supermarket)

Jolly Coffee & Late Breakfast $$

Kind of new, and rarely do I include a spot this new, but I sure did like the couple of times I stopped in! Hip and chic on a Cozumel side street with some very comfy chairs, it's a bit like a trendy café you might find in NYC. Next to The Hotel Flamingo, they offer lots of good coffees, espressos, teas, and the Eggs Benedict was wonderful, with a hollandaise sauce I couldn't quite put my finger on, but it was divine. My other visit I tried their breakfast burrito which was oozing with cheese, served hot and excellent.

Phone: 52-987-688-5089

(Calle 6, between Rafael Melgar and 5)

El Rincon De Addy $

A combination art gallery and breakfast nook, the charm here at El Rincon De Addy is endless. Owned by local artist Addy Bacelis, she is nearly always there acting as hostess and creating something with her paint brush. If the color and aromas don't draw you in, her engaging smile will. The sort of sweet taste of her Chaya and eggs, or the ham and eggs, even pancakes, the house omelet, or the chilaquiles with chicken or egg are all excellent choices. Maybe a 10-minute walk from town, it is so very well worth your time as this is a destination which every visitor to the island should make at least once. If you do, you'll be hooked! Great fruit smoothies as well, actually my last visit I had two!

Phone: 52-987-872-4198

(Near the corner of Miguel Hidalgo and Ave. 30)

El Coffee $

Just off the main drag is this wonderful and friendly little spot, El Coffee. Their bakery delights will be mentioned a tad more in-depth later, but the food here is excellent. For breakfast try the variety of Lattes, Cappuccinos, espressos, and full-bodied coffees to get your morning off to the right start. The indoor seating is just fine, they have AC, it is impeccably clean, and the staff could not be more friendly!

Aside from the selection of coffees, try the fruit plate, or their variety of omelets, bagels, and baguettes, like their smoked ham, tomato, and avocado baguette, all delicious. So, if you are in the mood for a dessert while on your morning breakfast stop, the cheesecakes, banana bread, and even a chocolate cake are just a sampling of their choices. Outstanding in every way.

Phone: 52-987-869-0456

(Calle 3, between R. Melgar and 5)

The Municipal Market (Mercado Municipal) $

You will find several little breakfast spots here at the municipal market, and when you are done with your breakfast, you will have the entire local market to stroll through where you will find fresh fruit, fresh fish, flowers, breads, and nearly anything you can imagine in a local market.

My personal favorite stop here for breakfast is Loncheria "Don Molis," but there are several and all are open-air, but covered from the elements. "Don Molis" is simple and with a homey Cozumel vibe. You will be dining with local families and the occasional ex-pat, all enjoying the local ambiance of this place. Huevos Rancheros, a variety of Quesadillas, a huge ham and cheese omelet with a side of potatoes, even pancakes and hearty breakfast burritos. As local as it gets for a nice Cozumel breakfast.

(Corner of A. R. Salas and 20)

Sucré Salé Café $$

Delicious, artisanal, and with a charming family and staff that operate this wonderful bakery and breakfast spot. You might as well be on the streets of Auvergne, France when entering this place. You may have gathered by now that I love Eggs Benedict, and I do, but it is also a great barometer of the quality of a breakfast spot when the chef nails the subtle nuances of this dish. They nail it here. The crispy French Toast is outstanding as well, but the bakery items are simply superb. Homemade breads, fruit tarts, warm muffins, pastries galore, crepes, croissants, cookies, jams, and amazing salads too. The folks here are artists, creating some of the best food and treats on the island.

Phone: 52-987-115-5968

(On 2, between 5 & 10)

Antojitos Doña Pili $

One of the most unique little buildings on the island (sort of like an igloo), and as authentic and simple Yucatecan food as you will find anywhere. The quesadillas are made with fresh homemade corn tortillas. The food here is inexpensive and excellent, though the menu is essentially limited to quesadillas, they are absolutely wonderful. Beans, real Oaxacan cheese, cactus, eggs, and a variety of other surprises, all cooked and prepared in their large oven indoors. For a taste of something very special on the island where you will find nothing but locals, Doña Pili is excellent.

Yes, they have coffee, a couple of cappuccinos as well, but the juices here may be the show-stopper. Lemonade with cucumber, a cucumber juice that is quite refreshing, chocolate liquado (kind of like thin chocolate milk), and several other options. Sit indoors or outside at one of the few comfortable benches. Typically closes around 1:00 p.m.

Phone: 52-987-869-1003

(Ave Coldwell just one block south of the airport road)

La Perlita $

Open daily from 8:00 a.m.–8:00 p.m., La Perlita is known on the island for their fresh seafood more than anything, but the breakfast here is excellent featuring old family island recipes. Unless you have your own transport, you will need a cab as it is about a 15–20 block walk from the ferry pier in Cozumel.

Chances are you will be dining here with mostly local families beginning their day. If you love black beans, these are some of the best! Their empanadas (sort of a fried turnover) are delicious with Dutch cheese, or several omelet choices such as their daily special, which will change of course, and the Fitness omelet featuring panela cheese, pepper and Chaya leaves (a Mayan green). Motulenos are a traditional breakfast dish with eggs on fresh tortillas, black beans, cheese, and any other number of ingredients. They are a featured breakfast fare here.

Phone: 52-987-869-8343

(At 65 and calle 10)

Blue Angel Dive Resort $$

It's a dive resort of course, but the food and views are excellent, and non-guests are more than welcome. I have had numerous wonderful breakfasts here, though Blue Angel is more known for its sunsets, dinners, and live evening music in a stunning location.

We're talking breakfast though, and the hustle and bustle in the morning with the divers all preparing their gear can be missed as you walk upstairs and sit down to enjoy the beautiful views. Start your morning with a pretty darn good Bloody and take your time here under the palapa roof. Breakfast baguettes, omelets served with potatoes, and usually, a side of bacon or sausage, or the Eggs Benedict is typically right on! If you're a fish lover, they have a Benedict with fish, it is excellent.

Phone: 52-987-872-0819

(On the main drag, just a couple minutes south of the Car Ferry pier)

Buccano's $$$

Relatively new on the island, but it would be an understatement to say this restaurant has taken Cozumel by storm. Everything here is outstanding with top-notch service as well. Breakfast, lunch, and dinner are served, and the views are breathtaking.

While this is high-end dining on the island, there is a very good reason as their kitchen staff is top-notch and meals are prepared with an artistic excellence that is near the top of the island's restaurant chain. Clean and with a tasteful tropical décor, the walls are hung with beautiful art and their furnishings are both traditional and artistic, you could meander the grounds here and feel as if you are in a tiny museum.

Some of the best scrambled eggs I have ever had might be Buccano's scrambled eggs, served on a Parmesan encrusted Crostini, prepared with sautéed fresh shrimp, and a pesto sauce draped over it all and spiced to perfection, it is divine. They offer chilaquiles stuffed with panela cheese (a Mexican white cheese), a red and green sauce, and poached eggs. A couple of omelets are on the menu and the bacon, avocado with Manchego cheese omelet has been my choice twice. For a more traditional Yucatecan selection, try their breakfast panuchos or if your appetite leans north of the border, the French Toast with a hint of coconut is amazing. Breakfast here includes a generous fruit plate, and either coffee or juice. This is one of the islands' best.

Phone: 044-987-114-5607
(A mile or so north of the Playa Del Carmen ferry pier on your left as you head north)

Beds and Friends Hostel $

This wonderful little spot has been on the island for a long time now, and there is a good reason why. Yes, it is a youth hostel, but all ages are welcome and greeted with smiles. The tiny outdoor kitchen is nearly always open and there are a few tables in the sand to enjoy the rustic, but always clean surroundings, where you will enjoy a quiet, fun, and different atmosphere for an island breakfast.

I make it a point to stop here several times each visit, either to take a nap in a hammock, have a cold beer on a hot day, or a simple meal, which is always good. I am not sure how this place ALWAYS manages to maintain such a wonderful staff, but the owners are doing something very right. The menu changes at times, and is somewhat limited, but there are always fresh eggs that can be prepared any way you like, fresh fruit plates, or excellent tacos. From simple bread, butter and jam, or fresh bread with Nutella, banana, and cinnamon, to chocolate pancakes with banana, a breakfast sandwich, or chilaquiles and omelets are all available here at one of the islands most charming little stops in a very quiet neighborhood.

Phone: 52-987-869-1820

(The southwest corner of calle 10 and 10)

The Maple Bakehouse $

Two locations on the island now, and I love them both, but I hope they never close the original! Some of the freshest and best pastries on the island, fresh bread, artisanal fruit preserves, and marmalades, this special place is an equally remarkable bakery and café. To me, the old location is more café and the new more shop/bakery, but both offer nearly the same.

Fresh juices, a coffee bar, fruit smoothies to die for, and my favorite Eggs Benedict on the island. The staff is always helpful, charming, and very knowledgeable about all the different products made fresh daily at The Maple Bakehouse. We will discuss later under "bakeries," but this a definite must stop for any connoisseur of quality baked goods. The breakfast crepes are something special.

Phone: 52-987-869-2418

(Either near the coast on the corner of 6 & 5, or east at their new location on 30, between 17 & 19)

Hotel Bella Caribe (and their partner restaurant Los Molcajetes) $

I mention Hotel Bella Caribe and their partner restaurant not only for the wonderful local breakfast cuisine but the weekly Sunday buffet is outstanding, economical and a place where your pesos will go a long way. Each Sunday morning, the buffet is set up in the hotel lobby where you will dine with nearly all local families, stopping in before or after church, amidst the color and array of flowers, tropical vines, and an old-world Mexican hacienda charm.

The family that owns this lovely place and their staff speak little English, but don't let that stop you. An endless supply of fresh fruit awaits you and at the grill, the cook will create any omelet you request and as many as you desire. The center buffet table is usually filled with fresh breads, pastries, and other surprises. A bottomless supply of juices is available, and we haven't even touched the 10–12 hot plates filled with breakfast dishes across the spectrum, but most are local Yucatecan recipes. Huevos Rancheros, chilaquiles, enchiladas, sweet potato chorizo hash, breakfast tostada fixings, black beans, various casseroles, and lots of tastes I have no idea what they are! I challenge anyone NOT to get their money worth here. This buffet is a special island treat that you rarely hear about, it is incredible.

(Ave. 30, a block south of the airport road)

Jeanie's Waffle House $$

I've lost track of how many years Jeanie's has been on the island, but it's a lot. An institution would be an understatement and it is far more than a waffle house and breakfast destination these days, but it is the breakfast we will focus on. Close to town, a few blocks south of the Playa Del Carmen ferry pier and directly across from the huge Mega supermarket, Jeanie's packs in a lot of cruisers and many expats living on the island. The views of the ocean are beautiful, and you can dine either inside or out.

It is not only waffles served here, though waffles are what has made this place famous. Chocolate chip waffles served with either banana, strawberry or blueberries, or even a waffle stuffed with pecans, the traditional Jeanie's waffle, and a waffle topped with white cheese, fried eggs, a ranchera sauce, and ham! As you might have gathered, I love my Eggs Benedict and Jeanie's does not disappoint. The breakfast menu is extensive and the Bloody Marys are usually divine. Everyone will find something on the menu, from their vegetarian omelet with celery, onions, mushrooms, green pepper and of course cheese, a traditional Arrachera thin steak with fried eggs on top, a ranchera sauce, served with beans, a simple continental breakfast or the Mexican light breakfast of juice, fruit, chilaquiles and either coffee or tea.

Phone: 52-987- 878-4647

(5 or so blocks south of the ferry pier, across from the Mega supermarket and on the water)

OVERALL DINNERS

So many of the relatively new restaurants in Cozumel have drifted away from the traditional island food offered here for so many years. It is a somewhat confusing, and exciting state of affairs for restaurants on the island trying to satisfy the tastes of travelers. Visitors are enjoying the many delightful dining options Cozumel now offers. With restaurant supplies far more available in Cancun, Playa Del Carmen, and even Cozumel than ever before, it has become easier to consistently procure foods that even 10–15 years ago were far more difficult to purchase. Some of the old standard island restaurants have adapted a bit to the international tastes desired by many of today's travelers, but most have stood their ground thankfully and continue to offer the delicious traditional food they have always served.

This is the nature of the development and growth of a travel destination like Cozumel. The mix of different styles and tastes in food has changed dramatically as the island has become more frequently traveled. Some wonderful island family-owned restaurants have suffered over the years while others have continued to do very well. Our dining suggestions bring to you a mix of all of the above and we will typically make a special note of an establishment if it is one of the many long-standing island vendors.

*You will see "ceviche" mentioned often in the upcoming pages, so it deserves some explanation. Served throughout the Yucatan but originating in either Peru or Ecuador depending on the historian, it is a marinated combination of lemon, vinegar, onions, tomato, and sometimes cilantro and lime, and many variations thereof. Then it will either have fish, conch, shrimp, lobster, octopus, or a combination of the above. Ceviche is typically served in a bowl or on a large platter and can be added to any dish or eaten alone with chips; it is delightful and will be on nearly all menus in Cozumel. Also, if you are not familiar with cilantro it is like a spicy parsley, and is the leaf of the same plant we get coriander from; coriander is the seed. Cilantro is often used in guacamole and many other local dishes.

Cozumel has a wide variety of outstanding restaurants. You can enjoy a meal for $2.00 or $100.00, or anywhere in between. Enjoy this long list and some of the best dinner spots on the island, there will be something for everyone!

Eat well, my friends . . .

El Moro $

As classic a Cozumel restaurant as there is. Set back in the neighborhoods of San Miguel, you will want to take a cab, but once you get there you will be greeted by some of the friendliest staff on the island. I am not exactly sure when they moved from their old location in town, but they have been in this spot for many years.

The margaritas are strong and delicious and their menu extensive. Traditional moles, mouthwatering Conchinita Pibil (slow cooked pork), an array of fajitas, burritos, and wonderful soups including a Cream of Asparagus, Lime Soup, and a Garlic Soup, with or without egg. El Moro is excellent for large groups, and their old family island recipes have brought visitors back time and again. The seafood platters are huge, try the excellent garlic shrimp. Very popular with expats, locals, the dive crowd, and even the occasional cruise ship group. If there is a wait. . . wait, the servings and food are well worth it.

If it is local seafood you are after, they will not disappoint. Save room for dessert as well because the coconut ice cream and cheesecake are a perfect way to end one of the most fun meals you will have when visiting Cozumel.

Phone: 52-987-872-3029
(At 75 bis, between 2 & 4)

New Especias $$

One of the most frequented authentic Italian restaurants on the island. Those who love an Italian experience when visiting Cozumel will make this remarkable destination a frequent stop. I have only visited here twice, and Italian is not my first choice, neither here nor at home, but the food here is amazing.

Romantic and elegant, and it was the welcoming entrance from the sidewalk which first caught my eye. The upstairs dining area is popular as it is open on two sides, creating an open-air tropical feel, even though it is a few blocks off the water, the sunsets can be beautiful.

The fresh pastas made on-site. While not being a pasta lover, I did have a stuffed lobster pasta and it was sensational. I have also sampled the lobster cooked in some sort of cognac sauce which was equally as exquisitely prepared and delicious.

I mention this place for so many reasons, but if you are looking for a special and romantic night out, or Italian food as if you were in Ancona, Italy, or for a lovely sunset and a very good bottle of wine, New Especias is traditional Italy in Cozumel.

Phone: 52-987-869-7947
(On 3 between 5 & 10)

Azul Madera $$$

Formerly Sal De Mar, and I am not sure why the name change, but it is the same uniquely excellent restaurant with international twists and turns, in a menu filled with surprises and excellence. For the wine snob, this is one of the islands choices for sure, and before we even get to the menu, I know some who will go here for the desserts alone. The somewhat contemporary layout offers several different rooms, each with sort of a unique setting. If looking for a particular spot to enjoy a meal here, and if it is your first time, it is advisable to maybe come in ahead of time, scope the place out and make a reservation, the staff is friendly and accommodating.

Cleverly lit, with art placed throughout, Azul Madera is part chic NYC and part bistro, but uniquely Azul Madera in Cozumel, Mexico. For an appetizer, I was wowed by the simple and tasty fried avocados with a touch of ginger, jalapenos, coriander (the seed of the cilantro plant), and minced onion, it was sensational. Being a hoisin sauce lover, I tried the Duck Tacos prepared with hoisin sauce and the duck was as well prepared as any I have had in the states. If any of you love duck, it can be hit or miss anywhere, but here it was perfectly prepared. They offer any number of uniquely flavored fresh fish options, with different homemade sauces and herb concoctions from a tomato and sweet pepper sauce, to white wine and chopped parsley, or a green olive sauce, and their Filet Mignon or New York Angus are prepared per request and are wonderful.

For the pizza lover, each pizza is a work of art. So, while you may wonder, they have a Yucatan pizza with like a crispy pork rind that is delicious and tender, blended with an Edam cheese, red onion, and peppers. Desserts include cheesecake, chocolate cake, brownies, lemon pie, and chocolate mousse!

Phone: 52-987-872-2708

(On 3, between 5 & 10)

Cielito Lindo $

My favorite time to visit this lovely little island restaurant is after the sun goes down, either for a couple of cold beers, a great margarita and the quaint sidewalk atmosphere that makes this place so fun. Oddly enough, I don't know if you can sit inside because each visit I am drawn immediately to one of the outdoor tables set amidst the potted plants and lush foliage. Cielito Lindo is a quiet evening or late night must if you are in search of an outdoor sidewalk café setting on the island.

Cielito Lindo offers Yucatecan food which is all quite simple and excellent. Chicken enchiladas, or a large and mouthwatering lobster burrito, and for the pulled pork lovers, the Mexican style Conchinita Pibil can be difficult to find in Cozumel if you are not familiar, but what they serve here is marinated and seasoned to perfection. Either as an appetizer or a full meal, their seafood ceviche alone is worth the stop.

Along with another place on the island which I will mention later, the Key Lime Pie here when available is yummy.

Phone: 52-987-869-2031

(NW corner of 5 & 3)

Sorrisi Restaurant Italiano $$$

Another of the islands go to restaurants for authentic Italian, a good wine selection, lovely atmosphere, and wonderful wood-fired thin Italian pizzas! Just off the main drag on the island, they open mid-afternoon, but it is evenings when this place hops. Sorrisi is well-known for its daily in-house prepared pasta, Caesar Salads, seafood dishes, and even their steaks, but it is the pizza I am most familiar with.

Apparently, this is how pizza is meant to be, delicious thin crust, from a wood-fired oven. Sorrisi prepares them just that way with sauces, high-quality cheeses, and spices to complement each offering they have. I may be a bit boring, but I love the pepperoni or the Hawaiian, simple as that!

Kind of a contemporary Italian/Mexican atmosphere, guests here can find a romantic corner or seating for a small group. Tremendous pride is taken at Sorrisi with each customer who walks through the doors and with each dish that is prepared in their kitchen, it is readily apparent at every turn when dining here. They even offer from what I understand are excellent Rib-eyes, Veal Chops, and New York Strips. Finding a true quality piece of steak in the Yucatan can be a task, but food is becoming more and more readily available each year for island restaurants.

Phone: 52-987-869-0960
(Calle 3, between Melgar and 5)

Buccanos $$

Part of a beautiful north end beach club, Buccanos is open for breakfast, lunch, or dinner, and all are excellent. I have never quite figured it out, but there is a gate a few hundred feet off the road, and I have never been charged by the attendant? Others tell me that there is a charge to enter, and it will be deducted from your bill, whatever, either way, it is well worth your visit. Relatively new on the island, and as mentioned earlier under "breakfast," the dining experience and the food here has taken this island by storm.

Tastefully appointed with art and paintings as you stroll the property, Buccanos is an experience far more than just the food, but the food is superb. I have only eaten here once for breakfast and once for dinner, so I will mention what I enjoyed and the highlights of their very creative menu. My dinner began with their shrimp ceviche served with guacamole and chips and it was excellent, as was the ice-cold Bohemia beer. My main course was the Blackened Fish Tacos and again I was not remotely disappointed. They came with guacamole, some sort of awesome coleslaw, orange chutney and grilled pineapple. I can certainly say that I have never had anything remotely like it, the meal was creative and absolute perfection.

The table next to me was served an appetizer of huge grilled shrimp that looked incredible and nosy as I am, I asked them about the salad that was brought to their table as well, it was a Lobster Caesar Salad with a generous ½ lobster tail.

Buccanos offers several different salads, all seemingly as creative as the next, subs, pizzas, and the Parmesan Chorizo Crusted Chicken Breast looked particularly inviting, but I had no more room.

The views are gorgeous, the staff and service are wonderful, and it is easily one of the prettiest dinner locations on the island. Good wine selection for sure and desserts include an assortment of ice cream, and cheesecake that is legendary, almost. This is an island must for the discerning diner not stuck on any one cuisine, but in search of a tropical setting, and quality at every turn. I will discuss the sister restaurant right next door, Shii Fu, in a bit.

Phone: 044-987-114-5607
(About ¾ of a mile north of the airport on the main road as you head to the north hotel zone)

Le Chef $$

Having recently moved from their old location in town to their new location facing the waterfront in late 2019, La Chef has a solid following on the island for their imaginative and delicious food. They are also a supporter of the island's vibrant art community, hosting galleries and displays of some of Cozumel's many fine artists.

Serving breakfast, lunch, and dinner, with a menu that can change daily and with seasonal specials, La Chef offers everything from Mediterranean, Thai, classic Mexican, and international cuisine across the spectrum. I have visited the old location and the new, but have never eaten at either. I stopped into the old location with a friend (Niurka Guzman) whose work was on display and failed to try the food. The new spot is beautiful with 6–8 tables in front facing the water, and available for a fine meal and a sunset, with an equal amount of seating in back with AC.

Excellent soups, creative salads, pasta, pizzas, sandwiches, seafood, and a wine list comparable to some of the best on the island. I understand the Lobster Bacon Sandwich and the Bloodys are excellent!

Phone: 52-987-878-4391

(On the main drag Rafael Melgar, between 4 & 6)

La Chardonnay $$

One of Cozumel's least discussed and cutest little restaurants, just 4 blocks off the beaten path of the Town Square. I have eaten here many times and rarely are there more than a handful of other guests, but it is quiet in the lovely back garden area, and simply one of the most delightful stops for dinner in Cozumel. There are a couple of tables on the front porch as you enter La Chardonnay, and several indoors, but it is the back area filled with plants, flowers, and trees that is the show-stopper here.

They offer pasta, pizza, salads, Mexican food, fresh ceviche, wonderful seafood, and even burgers, in a cozy backyard setting, second to just a few on the island. The Tropical Salad with crisp lettuce and other greens is served with fresh seasonal berries, peaches, beets, carrots, shrimp, and cheeses with a yogurt and mint dressing, it is amazing. The Europa Pizza comes with pineapple, pepperoni, ricotta cheese, black olives, and tomatoes, which is sort of a Hawaiian pizza, European style. Their fresh fish of the day will change by day obviously, and they offer a Deviled Shrimp entrée in sort of a mildly spicy pepper sauce smartly seasoned, or a house favorite is their Fajita Seafood Brandy Flambe served with fresh guacamole and black beans.

If you must, they have 2–3 burger options, but everything I have tried here is wonderful. The front porch is a favorite stop of mine early evenings for a cold beer or an excellent margarita as I end my daily research and take in the quiet surrounding neighborhood.

Phone: 52 987 872 1351

(On the corner of 7 & 5)

La Casa Del Mojito $

Tiny and unassuming, La Casa Del Mojito is the baby sister of the larger Cozumel icon, Wet Wendy's. Not a large restaurant by any means, as there are maybe 6 tables along the wall and also a long bar for a cocktail or one of their Cuban sandwiches. There are also 2–3 tables out front along the sidewalk. It is a late-night or early evening sandwich stop, with a great selection for the Mojito lover. Sample a cherry mojito, an Italian mojito with Frangelico (an Italian liqueur), or a Kiwi flavored mojito, or the favorite of the house, the chocolate mojito. If you are a cigar lover, here you will find what you can be assured is a true Cuban, and they offer a couple of specials to make that good Cuban smoke fairly affordable.

The chicken wings are great or share the Cuban Combo with a couple of friends, complete with wings, fries, tostones (fried plantain slices), deep-fried pork loins, celery, and the house dressing. The selection of 8 or so sandwiches includes the Cuban Special, which is a pressed pork leg with Manchego cheese and pickles, or the Chicken Strip sandwich with fried onions and Manchego cheese.

(On 5, between A. R. Salas and 3 sur)

El Palomar Restaurant $$

Set in an old island home with its secrets and mysteries within dating back to the early 1900s, El Palomar seems to be ever-changing but always excellent. Take in a stunning sunset on the old front porch with a cocktail from their endless repertoire, or sip a sample from their collection of mezcals, before dining at one of the islands very unique and fun spots. They are always showcasing the work of local artists and artisans, and aside from being a fine restaurant, this place is a reflection of Cozumel's past and present. From the building to the artwork and the island cuisine, it all wraps up into a delightfully smart dining experience on Cozumel.

The menu seems to change and evolve quite often, items come and go, but that is fine and it is the nature of many restaurants, fresh ideas and new twists keep things exciting. Sit out on the beautiful old front porch or indoors in one of three or so rooms, or belly up to the bar, there is not a bad seat in this place. I've enjoyed the seafood soup, both the lobster and shrimp empanadas, the rib eye and shrimp tacos on blue tortillas, and I have sampled the cold avocado soup, all were outstanding. Typically, I will sit at the bar though, and almost always order a margarita, no salt, and my meal of choice is almost always the seafood soup, I love it. El Palomar is wonderful for small groups of 10 or less, maybe more if you check ahead of time, and it is romantic as well for that special evening.

Phone: 52-987-120-2792
(Rafael Melgar on the north corner of 10)

Pancho's Backyard

An exquisite Hacienda setting with classic old-world Mexico décor, Pancho's Backyard is just beautiful. Inside the Los Cinco Soles complex across from the Malecon downtown, the restaurant is decorated with beautiful old furniture, wooden tables and chairs, art hanging from the walls throughout, potted plants, and 3–4 different dining areas. You could be in old town Mexico City or San Miguel De Allende, but no you are right here in the heart of Cozumel. The wait staff are all dressed in bright traditional Mexican clothing and could not be more pleasant.

The soups are divine, such as their Cream of Cilantro along with a host of salads, tapas (like an appetizer), a Mole Chicken, delicious Shrimp Brochetta (like a shish kebab), and the House fajitas could feed four. Romantic, or fun for a large group, Pancho's Backyard is Mexican elegance amidst interior gardens and tropical beauty.

Phone: 52-987-872-2141
(Across from the waterfront between 8 & 10)

La Clasica $

Wow, La Clasica is new to the island in 2019 and is owned by the same innovative group who have opened Kinta, Kondessa, Cuatro Tacos, and one more on the island that I forget. A short walk from the town square, La Clasica is just that, a classic and quaint sidewalk cantina, like a Mexican bistro.

Adjacent to the sidewalk are several tables for outdoor seating, covered with a canopy, and indoors there is seating for maybe 20. Traditional Mexican music quietly entertains diners and the food is conducive to sharing with a small group or couple. The menu is small and could be described as a modern and imaginative twist maintaining the simplicity of Mexican street food.

A homemade habanero sauce, great guacamole, and a variety of salsas are served with each dish, the habanero sauce is out of this world.

The Shrimp Enchiladas are wonderful as are the variety of tostadas and tacos. Order several items and share them among friends as nothing is too expensive. I particularly enjoyed a tostada with tuna, sesame seeds, and an Asian eel sauce. If you are a Mexican street corn fan, this is your place.

Ingredients and menu items will change depending upon availability. The selection of crafted cocktails is as creative as their food or simply enjoy a classic mojito or margarita.
(Ave. 5 between 4 & 6)

La Cocay $$

One rarely hears of this long-standing and top Cozumel restaurant on social media sites, but La Cocay is certainly one of the islands finest. Mediterranean food yes, but La Cocay is much, much more. Within this past year, they updated their seating quite a bit, adding a lovely outdoor space and AC to the inside.

A nice wine list, wonderful steaks, traditional Yucatecan cuisine as well, even a couple of choices of burgers and lamb chops perfectly prepared to your request. La Cocay is really more of a late-night experience, 9:00 p.m. is early here! The restaurant is located a short walk from the town square in a lovely old island building, but once here, you are in a quiet neighborhood and will enjoy a dining experience those in the know have kept to themselves for decades.

I love scalloped potatoes, La Cocay surprised me with them as they can be a rarity down here. Theirs are excellent and are served as a side with several items. The spaghetti and ravioli are supposed to be superb and the fish of the day is always seared and served to perfection, but the creativity of this place is all through their menu. Tuna Sashimi tapas, with pesto (homemade) and a wasabi infused mayonnaise, or the sautéed shrimp with a not too hot Cajun spice, served with an Asian inspired pear salad, and a slow cooked duck wrapped in tortilla rolls with glazed pineapple, honey, chipotle, and a salsa with corn, tomato pepper, and mango. This is just a small sampling of how creative this place can be.

La Cocay is one of those awesome places on the island that just keeps ticking, under the radar.
Phone: 52-987-872-5533
(Calle 8, between 10 & 15)

El Abuelo Gerardo $

Another under the radar local restaurant that is often lost in the restaurant shuffle, El Abuelo Gerardo has been serving up a mix of island and traditional Yucatecan dishes for years on Cozumel. It is especially popular for lunch and dinner, and popular for locals, tourists, and the cruise ship crowd alike. Located a block off the town square, the food and atmosphere are wonderful in a sort of large setting just off the sidewalk.

Complimentary chips and guacamole are served as you are seated, the service is always fast and friendly, and while sometimes this place is shrugged off by a few, I have always thought that it ranks up there with all the other long-time island establishments. Their seafood platter is always a good choice for a group and depending on the season can be a combination of the fish of the day, conch, lobster, octopus, shrimp, and any other number of surprises. The ceviche will not disappoint and their guacamole is excellent. The chicken and shrimp tacos are yummy, sizzling hot beef fajitas and the refried beans served with nearly everything is a treat.

Great for large groups especially, business lunches or even parties, El Abuelo Gerardo will handle it.

Phone: 52-978-872-1012
(On 10 ave. norte, between Juarez and calle 2)

Kelley's Sports Bar and Grill $$

So, the past few years have seen some ups and downs here since Gene sold the place, inconsistency, maybe a lack of commitment by the owner, I'm not sure, but it is still my favorite spot on the island for a Packer victory! The staff changes often, but hello and good luck with that in a restaurant driven place like Cozumel. Regardless, they are always extremely friendly and somehow the same good food comes out of the kitchen, never have I been disappointed.

The food is nothing fancy and it is gringo food, but it is consistently good. Kelley's is a place to watch international sports, without the interference of loud music blaring, if you request. The ribs are always excellent and a favorite here (there are 2 sizes), the burgers served with either fries or potato salad are delicious, as are the chicken or beef quesadillas. If your taste buds continue to lean north, there are not many spots on the island where you will find a hearty Reuben sandwich with sauerkraut or a tasty Hot Pastrami sandwich on rye, but you will find them here.

My favorite items here have always been the Chicken Curry or the big ole Beef Burrito. Bar food, absolutely, and as good as any bar food I have tried in the states. I certainly hope Kelley's gets through their road bumps, as I for one will continue to patronize as long as my Packers are on, the tequila flows, and my Chicken curry is hot.

Phone: 52-987-878-4738
(Ave. 10, just north of A. R. Salas)

Ohana $$

I finally stopped in Ohana for the first time during one of my 2019 trips to Cozumel, and what an absolute joy! I dare say I have only visited once, but I will be back. First of all, as you walk by you can never imagine, how lovely and spacious this place is on the inside, especially the stunning outside garden area in the back. It is one of my new favorites on the island. I need to reiterate, the small building this place is in is gorgeous, but you just need to step inside to get the real feel. Live music most weekends, and while the menu is a mix of Caribbean delights, the Chicago Deep Dish to me was the draw that particular evening.

I was alone and ordered the small pizza with lobster I think, and I had it for breakfast and a bit for lunch the next day! Apparently, the pizzas are all made from scratch, and I didn't mind the odd 40-some minute wait whatsoever. I scanned the menu, strolled around a little, had a couple of beers and a margarita (as usual with no salt), yes, all 3. The pizza was oozing with cheese, the crust wasn't thick like I have had in the past, but it was delicious. I opted out of the Peanut Butter Tequila, but local legend has it that it is something quite remarkable, maybe someday.

Other menu items included burgers, 2–3 different ceviches, a lobster burger which I will for sure try next time, and a Coconut Shrimp which I was told was a must. Nachos, fajitas, a shrimp burger, fresh seafood choices, and lots more good-looking treats.

One rarely hears a bad word about Ohana. A short 5-minute walk from the town square away from the buzz of the town.
(Ave. 5, between 6 & 8)

Guido's

My motto when writing these guides has always been consistency, consistency, consistency. In Guido's own words, they say something quite similar about their ability to grow and evolve since 1978 when they first opened, "time tested restaurant qualities," and that is exactly what defines this remarkable Italian Restaurant. I don't pretend to be some lover of Italian food, I rarely indulge, and not because it hasn't been incredible when I have tried it, it is just that my taste buds carry me elsewhere. It is the pizza I have come here for. All of this spot's true excellence, I will leave to the rest of you.

Just look at some of these menu items, and all are created by a classically trained staff. Pastas include the Frutti de Mare with black linguini, octopus, scallops, fresh tomato sauce, shrimp, cream and cognac, or the Pappardelle with mascarpone, portobello, and Mozzarella, or Yvonnes Salad which is a mix of barley, arugula, tomato, lime, basil, pistachio, and mint. An appetizer of calamari sautéed with garlic, guajillo, and a pepper purée, or the Osso Buco, a slow cooked braised pork shank, with saffron risotto. I can only imagine what it takes to pull off this type of a menu in a place like Cozumel. It is a desire to be the best, and that is what Guido's always reaches for.

There is a reason why the menus here are seasonal and daily at times, I assume it is the availability of the finest ingredients and the difficulty in procuring some at certain times of the year.

They are known for their sangria and one of the best wine collections on the island. The back-garden area is just stunning, quiet, partially covered from the elements, and the lush flowers, tree cover, and tropical foliage are captivating. Excellent desserts and flambés will complement what will surely be a special meal at a very special place. I won't bother to mention the pizza I ALWAYS order every time I visit, it will minimize all that is good about Guidos. The pizza is wonderful!
Phone: 52-987-872-0946
(Rafael Melgar, between 6 & 8)

Los Arcos $

A very simple, clean, and marvelous local taqueria. They do not serve much here but tortas, tacos, and a great burrito if you ask, try the chicken burrito! This is one of several small taquerias I will discuss here under dinners, and most will also be discussed later as well. Tacos pastor, sausage, chicken and smoked pork, or tortas with ham, shrimp, chicken, steak, and anything else they have available. The sauces are delish, cheese is available, and the guacamole is one of the very best. No alcohol, just juices, bottled water, and soda. Nice array of plenty of tables with room for nearly any large group.

Phone: 52-987-119-8121

(Ave. 30, between 5 & 7)

Los Moros Del Morrito $

Nearly legendary on this island and for very good reason. Just look for the yellow pillars at the entrance, and find your way inside an old-time island family-run restaurant. Traditional Yucatecan food, created with love, and everything is fresh here. Speaking of incredible guacamole, they have it. It amazes me the widely different qualities of guacamole on this island considering EVERYONE serves it, and only a handful are truly excellent.

Definitely order the lemonade to go along with whatever you select on the fairly large menu, none of which has ever disappointed me. A cab is probably best, but it really isn't that long of a walk from town, 20 minutes or so. Any cab will know where this is.

Of the 6–7 times I've stopped in here, I nearly always have a bowl of the lime soup, with shredded tender chicken and vegetables to get started. If I am alone, I won't order the Shrimp Fajitas, but when with a friend, nearly always! The chili rellenos are great, as is the conch ceviche, or any of their ceviches, and typically they have the traditional slow cooked pork Conchinita Pibil available, especially in the evenings. Los Moros Del Morrito serves a large selection of tacos, burritos, enchiladas, and other specialties as well. Enjoy one of the island's best.

Phone: 52-987-871-6512

(Ave. 35, between 3 and Adolfo Lopez Mateo)

Casa Denis $

The longest-standing island restaurant was also mentioned in our breakfast section. This is traditional island and Yucatecan food from a family that has been operating on the island for nearly 70 years, and while the food has changed a bit, the recipes and traditions have stayed the same, for the most part. The most fun about a visit to Casa Denis for dinner is that you are sitting out on the southeast walkway of the town square pedestrian walk and enjoying some of the best island dishes on Cozumel, watching the throngs of people stroll by and hopefully enjoying one of their sensational margaritas.

This is not designer food, it is simply seafood, great soups, and a wonderful Cozumel night out. Thick bean soup, a Mayan inspired Cream of Spinach Soup, tortas from ham and cheese, to egg and sausage, cheese empanadas thick and moist, fish and Mayan pork tacos, Chile Rellenos with shrimp or cheese, and the fish of the day prepared any way you desire or shish kebabs skewered with seasonal fish, shrimp, lobster and available veggies, and guacamole that stands with the best.

Casa Denis, experience delightful dining and history.

Phone: 52-987-872-0067

(The southeast walkway heading east from the town square)

Sharky's Pub $$

Formerly referred to as The Pub, in town, the gang has moved south to the Villablanca Dive Resort and opened up as Sharky's, after the shark above the sign at the hotel. The vibe is totally different, but the food is the same. The old building was a lovely structure, but nowhere near as old as you would think, and it was a deteriorating structural nightmare.

So, for now, the horseshoes are gone (it wasn't an official length anyway, short by like 5"), pool table is gone as well, but I am sure as things evolve in this new location, some of the old games and charm will return. For now, relax in the pool and get acquainted with a new environment. For those of you that aren't familiar with the menu, let me give you a reminder as it is a combination of British fare, gringo food, and a few other surprises, all brought to you by Chris, one of the most gracious South African hosts on the island!

The authentically delicious Indian Chicken Curry has been my choice from when The Pub first opened 7–8 years ago, but the menu offers burgers, like the Bacon/Cheeseburger with fries, tacos, quesadillas, ceviche, nachos, fajitas, the typical good local fare. It is here where the menu separates itself from the Cozumel pack, with offerings including a wonderful BLT (heavy on the bacon), a Philly Cheese Sub, Beer Battered British Fish and Chips, English Pot Pies, an occasional excellent meatloaf, and a Seafood Lasagna that is stunningly good.

Now serving breakfast, lunch, and dinner.

Phone: 52-987-101-9994

(A couple of miles south of the ferry pier on the grounds of the Villablanca Hotel)

Cerveceria Punta Sur $$

The island's first microbrewery as of 2019, and while beer is primary here as well as some salads, empanadas and a few other items available on the menu, the food is really about the wood-fired pizzas made on site. I sampled 3–4 of the 7 some odd beers available and loved the Amber Ale and the American IPA. I downed 2 IPA's as I waited for my pizza and an Amber Ale as I ate it!

So, the long bar greets you as you enter, along with 7 small tables for two, maybe 8 along the wall. In the back by the pizza oven, there are 3–4 tables outdoors. My ONLY complaint is the bar chairs are incredibly uncomfortable, otherwise, this place is way fun.

I believe there are 10 pizzas, and being alone at the time, I was only able to sample 2 during my visits, most of them came back to my room with me for consumption later. They are all handmade and all use Mozzarella. I did not try the ever-popular Lionfish (an invasive fish that is apparently causing more damage to the fisheries than I think), but I loved both the Punta Sur and the Nacional pizzas, both were outstanding!

Phone: 52-987-111-8642

(Ave. 10, between A. R. Salas and 3)

Pepe's $$$

Since the mid-'60's, in a few different locations and having settled into the current beautiful spot for easily 20 years, Pepe's was the original elegant steak house on the island. Step upstairs for an astonishing meal, especially if you are in the mood for a great steak and a sunset, or just watching the lights of the boats and cruise ships at night on the water.

Pepe's has evolved over the years, astonishingly to meet the needs and desires of international travelers while maintaining their core values here, it is beautiful and juggling the needs of visitors as well. Today you will find Thai inspired salads, a tremendous Caesar Salad, pastas, fresh fish prepared as you wish, and steaks that have been perfected for you over decades. Along with an excellent wine and champagne selection, possibly the best on the island, flaming coffee desserts, a selection of sides including roasted asparagus and delectable mashed potatoes, the Angus Fillet, Rib Eyes, and New York Strip steaks may be Cozumel's premier choice.

A Cozumel tradition of history and excellence.
Phone: 52-987-872-0213
(Rafael Melgar at the corner of A. R. Salas)

Shii Fu $$$

For the visitor in search of an Asian inspired theme and menu, this is for sure your choice. Next to Buccano's, in the same complex, the setting and the view here are stunning. Shii Fu is only a couple of years old and while I may be going out on a limb, they seem to have the staying power and food to find a home here on the island for a good long time.

I've only had one experience here, and besides the fact that they offer a fun change of pace on the island, the service is impeccable and is a wonderful complement to Buccanos. Granted I am a Thai fan, I didn't find any real Thai food here, the place seems to specialize in Japanese recipes. The Sashimi rolls were delicious and apparently, the difference between Sushi and Sashimi is that Sashimi uses no vinegar rice, but whatever, they only use the freshest fish of the day and they were wonderful. I sampled the shrimp Shii Fu roll as well and while yummy, it was the glazed house duck that got my attention, some sort of a marinade citrus sauce and perfectly prepared duck, it was astonishing!
Phone: 52-987-114-5607
(About ¾ of a mile north of the airport road. Look for the sign and for Buccano's)

Kinta $$

The sister restaurant to Kondessa, La Clasica, and others, Kinta is unique on its own and sensational in every way. As you enter, there is seating immediately on your left (check out the cool masks on the right along the wall as you enter) or proceed a bit further to a small bar, but if it isn't raining, you will want to sit in the back amongst the lush foliage, draped soft lights and candles, it is beautiful.

I was told to try the fall off the bone ribs and the Lobster Flat Bread, by nearly everyone I spoke with, but I chose to go a different direction. I did sit in the back though and it is fun to watch the cooks in the open kitchen, preparing the various dishes. For a romantic dinner, this place would be a prime choice. I didn't see a large wine selection but then again, I am not much of a wine drinker, the sangria though was quite good.

My meal this last stop consisted of the Seafood Lasagna, and for starters, I tried the flatbread with pesto, tomatoes, and Oaxacan cheese. Both were simply wonderful. The desserts carried out to various tables looked really good, but I had no more room. This is a restaurant owned by a local group of restaurateurs who seem to do no wrong. Kinta is special, low key, and oozes with a tropical vibe. Occasionally there is live music.

Phone: 52-987-869-0544

(Ave. 5, between 2 & 4)

Kondessa $$

Maybe a bit fancier than Kinta, with a large back garden under a spreading Ceiba tree with lit lanterns randomly hanging from the branches of the tree's magical canopy. I will normally sit at the palapa covered bar actually and sip on one of my favorite island margaritas, or a cold beer and an appetizer, or the Lobster Enchiladas which are amazing. If in the mood for a burger, they serve an excellent burger with a slice of pineapple and a small salad with cheese and nuts. The lovely bar serves as the entrance to Kondessa's charm and beauty.

The food is traditional Mexican fare and recipes, which the kitchen staff takes to a different level of elegance and presentation. If you have a special date, take him or her here, it is beautiful, and the tables seem to be spaced out far enough apart for a quiet evening. A large group would work as well, they will accommodate any request as the seating area is fairly expansive.

The churros for dessert are divine. Another success by this very in tune group of investors and restaurateurs! Soft live music typically on the weekends and during the high season.

Phone: 52-987-869-1086

(Ave. 5, between 5 & 7)

Casa Mission $$

Very elegant in an old-world way, as a meal at Casa Mission is like dining in a private hacienda somewhere in the mountains of central Mexico. Everything here from the napkin holders, to the art adorning the walls, is reflective of Mexican culture and the fine family that owns this beautiful property. And what a property it is, it takes up an entire city block on the eastern side of town. Stroll through the grounds before or after your dining experience here, they are a portrait in a way of Cozumel history. The grounds are a collection of potted plants, trees of all sizes, fountains, small palapas, a lawn, paved walkways, all surrounding the seating areas of the restaurant which for the most part are the front and south porches. You feel as though you are dining in a beautiful family home.

My highlight when visiting has always been the Veracruz Style Fish Fillet. Veracruz style is a blend of Spanish and Mexican influence dating back centuries. The homemade salsa on the fillet is delicious and it is served over rice with a crisp salad of greens and your choice of dressing. The Black Bean soup is a nice way to start or the Caesar salad served with delectable chunks of tender chicken. The recipes here stick to traditional Mexican roots and include Garlic Shrimp, fajitas, pork chops, and a couple of different steaks, excellent fish, and mixed ceviches, as well as many other items.

This is elegance and tradition in Cozumel.

Phone: 52-987-872-1641

(Corner of Juarez-and Ave 55)

Pescaderia San Carlos $

Authentic as authentic is, this is one of the best traditional seafood restaurants in Cozumel. Family owned and operated by gracious hosts who treat locals, expats, and the smart tourist to some of the island's best food and hospitality. Fresh, fresh, fresh, and not only is San Carlos a restaurant, but it serves as a fish market as well, but just walk in the door to the right and you will be dining in the family's front yard basically, as they live right behind the seating area.

You will need a cab to reach here, or a healthy 25-minute walk from the town square, and if you do come by cab, they will call you one upon completion of your meal. Tortillas are available for purchase as is the fish from the market, by the kilo, and if you prefer the delicious whole fried fish on the menu, you can select any particular fish fresh from the cooler. Seafood and shrimp quesadillas, fish or shrimp tacos, a seafood soup filled to the brim with chunks of whatever is available fresh that day, and the ceviches (a large or small platter are available) are among the best you will find on the island, which is a strong statement! Pan-fried fish fillets, or breaded fillets, and everything is served with their homemade proprietary slaw and rice. Opens at 11:00 a.m. and closes at 6:00 p.m., so this is an early dinner option. Cold beers and excellent strong margaritas are available.

Phone: 52-987-872-7440
(Calle 3 and biz 55)

La Perlita $$

Another of the island's premier locally run seafood destinations that simply cannot be missed. Open daily from 8:00 a.m.–8:00 p.m., just look for the palapa roof and wooden post entrance. A bit off the beaten path, but once again, if you aren't up for a 25-minute walk from town, any taxi will know the location and the hosts will call you a cab when your experience here is completed. La Perlita is mostly frequented by locals who know a good thing, and while this is not fancy dining, it is extremely nice, clean and the staff is very attentive. This is pure Cozumel dining the way it used to be.

Ok, so the margaritas are fantastic in this old family home converted into a restaurant, let me make that clear, they are excellent! Deemed invasive, the Lionfish on the menu here and around the island is one of their most popular items, I have never tried it, but it is wonderful. The ceviche is amazing, and the large platter will easily serve 4–6. Incredible lobster choices in season are prepared perfectly, and my choice is usually the stuffed fish fillet with all kinds of seafood treats inside, served with rice and homemade slaw. The shrimp fajitas are to die for and will feed 2–4. For dessert, the lime pie is special.

Phone: 52-987-869-8343
(Ave 65 and 10)

The Lobster House (and Fernando's Lobster House next door, all family) $$

Kind of by itself north of town, this is again one of the island's oldest restaurants. The "original" Lobster House moved out here from town years ago, and it was several years ago that the owner's son opened Fernando's directly next door. It's all in the family, because the owner's wife sold so much Key Lime Pie out of the restaurant, that a few years ago, she opened a place of her own directly next door to the north named appropriately, The Key Lime Pie Factory. I love Key Lime Pie and hers is exquisitely smooth and not too sweet.

So anyway, lobster is not all they sell here but it is certainly the focus. One can sit in the front where you will find a tiny bar, but the funky and lush jungle foliage in the back is where you want to be. Yes, there can be skeeters and they do burn citronella candles, but if they are bothering you, they will provide you with a spray. You can select your own lobster tail, and they actually prefer that and will charge by weight. The margaritas are excellent and the bar selection overall is pretty good.

The Shrimp Chowder is thick and can be a meal in and of itself, and the grilled grouper, fried or barbequed shrimp, or a Red Snapper stuffed with shrimp and slathered in a not too consuming homemade white sauce are marvelous choices. Most dishes come with select veggies and rice. Even the BBQ Chicken when on the menu, is awesome if you are just not in the seafood mood. Don't forget the Conch Soup and for sure do not forget mamas scrumptious Key Lime Pie.

Phone: 52-987-107-3116

(About 2.5 miles north of the airport road, hard to miss at they are all alone and across from the Westin)

La Conchita Del Caribe $

Yet again, this is another of the fabulous family restaurants that remind me of this island 45 years ago. Outstanding is an understatement, friendly as can be and if you want to have dinner here, come early as they close around 7:30–8:00 p.m. Look for the name on the orange front, painted light green below and unless you have a vehicle or feel like a 30-minute walk, take a cab.

It is quite simple, but very clean and welcoming with checkered red and white tablecloths and comfortable straight back wooden chairs. Chips and Pico de Gallo will be delivered to your table upon your arrival, have a cold beer or juice and contemplate your order, everything is delightful. If it is a whole fried fish, they will have you select from the cooler, but much more awaits you. The black beans which come with almost every meal are a favorite, and if you are in a group or family, the Seafood Platter will easily serve 3–4 and consists of lobster, fish, squid, conch, octopus, shrimp and maybe some other surprises. Nearly all meals also come with a salad, or veggies, and do not miss the amazing guacamole and fresh crisp chips.

The Yucatan style pork chops are tender, or the coconut shrimp, very generous lobster, and the skewered mixed seafood are always a favorite of mine.

Not a secret by any means, La Conchita Del Caribe is simple and outstanding!

Phone: 52-987-869-1218

(Ave. 65, between 13 and 15)

La Mission $$

Overlooked by some, but the place is always busy, very pretty with sort of an artificial stream running through it, and I love the food. It can get a tad loud on a busy night, but the setting is really quite lovely. The floors are varying and unusual combinations of inlaid stone, only adding to the quirky and tropical atmosphere of this long-time island establishment. Walk carefully over the small footbridge and you will see one of the prettiest entrances ever to a bathroom!

Plenty of room for large groups with ample offerings of seafood, chicken, traditional Mexican dishes from Stuffed Chile Peppers to a variety of fajitas. Fresh tossed salads, pretty good steaks, and a lively, fun atmosphere.

Phone: 52-987-879-0032

(A.R Salas, near 5)

Benitos $$

Another island stop one rarely hears discussed, but it is one of my favorite Cozumel locations. A bit out of the way, but when I am cycling town or doing research, I nearly always visit this funky and quiet little place. Sometimes for a cold beer, or a great margarita and occasionally my go-to for wood-fired pizza. Outdoor seating is available in front along the sidewalk, on the front patio, in a small courtyard, or you can choose to sit in what I think are 3 different rooms inside. Either way, Benitos is so pleasant and always friendly. Tucked away on a corner, a bit of a trek from town, but an easy cab ride or a 20-minute walk will get you there.

Hours are theoretically 11:00 a.m.–11:00 p.m., but depending on the season, they will open anywhere from 11:00 a.m.–3:00 p.m. realistically. Benitos serves breakfast, lunch, and dinner. Touted as an Italian restaurant with pastas, fettuccini, spaghetti, and several lasagnas, it is the pizzas and calzones here that draw the most attention, as do the empanadas.

They will probably make you any selection you request, but I normally opt for the small Jamaican or Tahiti pizza, because they are delicious, and I love pineapple! The Jamaican comes with bacon, sweet red peppers, and the Tahitian with ham, and both with pineapple and lots, and lots of cheese. Look for a cool building on the southwest corner with interesting wrought iron work along the roof line, the hanging sign, and the gate. Benito's is something very different on Cozumel.

Phone: 52-987-869-0914

(Ave Xel-Ha, and Ave 50 sur)

GREAT LOCAL, TACOS AND CASUAL CUISINE

So much of the joy of these places is the simple atmospheres, the unique side sauces, fresh chips, different salsas, pico de galos, outstanding guacamoles, and the fact that these are all typically long-time island families sharing old island recipes with you. These will often be some of the best memories and food you will have on your trip. Dine with locals, expats, and frequent visitors who know the secrets of these wonderful establishments.

Los Seras $

Usually opening by 6:00 each evening the spit of pork will be cooking, and there will be prepping of the pastor. Tacos Al Pastor is a favorite here, as well as any number of tacos, tortas, and even pizzas. I have had the pizza a couple of times and the crust was thick, it was not my favorite, but their tacos are excellent. This place stays busy until late, they do not serve alcohol. Los Seras is a bit out of town, but not really, it is about a 15-minute walk from the square, and after a meal here, enjoy the shops and life along one of the islands busiest streets.

Phone: 52-987-100-7848

(Ave. 30 and J.M. Morelos, on the northwest corner)

Diego's Tacos $

Amazing, perfectly simple, authentic, unassuming, and right across the street from the airport! Each visit, my first and last stop on the island is for 3 tacos from Diego's, and a lemonade. After customs, I'll step outside, grab a beer at the airport, and walk the 3 minutes directly across the street, just look for the red canopy covering on the other side of the roundabout.

Fish, shrimp, beef and chicken tacos, with their incredible homemade garlic habanero sauce, superb guacamole, a couple of side sauces and crisp chips are what you can look forward to. The ambassador for this tiny place is Erik, and with his mother doing the cooking and his sister at times helping out, they serve up some of the most delicious food on the island. There are only 5–6 tables, and the hours depending on the season are 9:00 a.m.–5:00 p.m.

Sign the large board as you enter or leave and leave your mark on this very special little place.

Phone: 52-987-564-9802
(On Ave. 65, right across from the airport)

Taqueria Rafa $

Rarely does one hear of this little spot mentioned, yet it is a secret that should get out! Impeccably clean and friendly, and owned and operated by a husband and wife team that know all too well the secrets of simple and exquisite Yucatecan dishes. The hours are a little odd, typically lunch runs from 11:00 a.m–2:00 p.m. or so, then shopping and a little break and they will open again late afternoon until around 9:00 p.m.

There isn't a whole lot of room, 7–8 tables, but take a short 10-minute walk from the town square into this quiet neighborhood and get ready for delicious. The menu can change from time to time, but the chicken soup seems to always be available and it is some of the best you will ever have. Chunks and strips of tender chicken, and just so perfectly spiced. While they have a steady assortment of tacos, soups, tortas, and other surprises, even tamales at times, it is the salsas that set this place apart. From extremely hot, to perfectly mild with just the right hint of whatever it is that sets each sauce apart, they are all wonderful and Rafa (Rafael) will be sure

in his own way, that you know darn well what is way hot and what isn't. This place is very special for the Mexican food "foodie."

(On 10 norte, between 10 & 15)

Asadero El Billy $

A barbeque spot like few others, for 20 years this place has rocked central San Miguel. It may not look like much but give it a shot because you will not regret it if you are at all a grilled meat lover. With their proprietary seasonings, Asadero El Billy provides in house meals (only 4 tables, maybe 5) and the carry-out clientele is beyond steady. This is more than just barbequed meats, though they are certainly the focus, the baked beans, black beans, baked potatoes, whole grilled onions, fresh corn tortillas made in house, and their coleslaw are served with each meal and are all available for carry-out as well.

If you like ribs, these are amazing, as is the roasted chicken (1/2 or whole), pork brochette (slow roasted pork), roasted potatoes, a wide array of roasted sausages, all cooked over a series of charcoal grills. Rarely have I experienced ribs this tender, and the sauces are a perfect complement and will not overwhelm the amazing taste of the ribs. Tacos or tortas can be made for you with any of the daily prepared meats. If you are unsure of what to order, they will provide different size sampler plates, with a ton of food! Open usually 11:00 a.m.–5:00 p.m.

Phone: 52-987-800-0711

(Ave. 65 and 19)

Los Tacotales (Formerly Los Otates) $

For years Los Otates has been one of the favorite taco spots on the island fairly close to town, and they have just changed their name. It's funny because the old sign is the same, they just added some letters over the old and voila, "Los Tacotales."

This is a fun place, no-frills, wonderful tacos al pastor, chicken and pork especially, but tortas, excellent guacamole and chips, and cold beer with a somewhat limited bar, which is surprising enough for a little place. They serve burritos, but I have never tried them. For me, it is typically a cold beer and chicken tacos, a side of guacamole, and whatever the variety of salsas they provide, some hot and some not, but ask first! Open 11ish till late.

Phone: 52-987-120-1076

(Ave. 15, between A. R. Salas and 3 sur)

Taco El Sitio $

An old Cozumel classic where nearly all the locals stop, open from 8ish to around 1:00 p.m. daily. Strictly tacos and tortas, not a fan of the tortas, but I do love the shrimp or fish tacos. They have a wonderful selection of sauces, fairly limited but excellent.

The chips are crisp, guacamole is really good and if you want simple and quick, you will find it here. El Sitio has been serving up food for years here, people love it and it fills up early in the morning.

(On 10, between 6 & 8)

El Pique $

On the busy Ave. 30 (J. Coldwell), El Pique is one of several great old tacos and torta spots along the street. Opening around 5:00 and staying open late, they serve both in-house and carry-out. Street tacos at their finest, tortas, fajitas, excellent guacamole, and a selection of a few cold beers. A local's place for sure, and nothing wrong with that, they always know a good thing.

The menu is extensive and in Spanish, but the staff is helpful if you need help. I always lean toward an order of guacamole (the large one) and a selection of chorizo (sausage) and arrechera steak with cheese. The tortillas are fresh, the chips are the same, and for an authentic, entertaining, street-side Mexican evening, El Pique is one of the ideal spots. Tacos are a bit over a dollar apiece, and the place is a bargain with comfortable seating. Very popular especially between 8:00–10:00 p.m.

(Ave. 30, between B. Juarez and 2 norte)

Chilangos

Extremely popular with the locals and those in the know, and one of the few places that serve tamales on a regular basis, but they run out quick. Along the lively Ave. 30, they open late afternoon and are very busy well into the night. Great street tacos of all kinds and Huaraches, kind of a corn dough fried turnover with beans, onions, and potatoes, and they offer them with a variety of meats.

Very authentic with a buzzing take-out business all evening. My choice here is the tacos, but the chicken and cheese quesadillas are delicious. Like most local street vendors, Chilangos has a nice selection of agua frescas, an NA beverage often with fruit or even hibiscus flower. Chilangos has watermelon, pineapple, papaya, and a few others, they are so refreshing. This is one of the locals' most popular restaurants on this stretch.

Phone: 52-987-872-3072
(Ave. 30, just south of 3 sur)

Señor Iguanas $

Of the 7 or so little beach bars (some aren't so little anymore) on the east side of the island, Señor Iguanas is probably the smallest. Just south of the transversal road once you have reached the east side, you will see Señor Iguanas. There is a small bar with maybe 5 stools and a seating area of about 15 tables, all with an open panoramic view of the Caribbean. The guacamole and especially the shrimp tacos are amazing, not to mention the margaritas. There isn't a whole lot to do here except take pictures and hang for a while, but a shrimp taco stop will be well rewarded!

Phone: 52-987-105-6344
(Just south of the transversal road on the east side of the island)

Las Palmas $

A marvelous selection for a late lunch or early dinner, Las Palmas has a complete menu of Yucatecan family recipes passed down through generations. Fresh salads, guacamole, grilled pork, chicken and seafood dishes, soups, and a multitude of individual plates or larger dishes of samplers for groups or families.

Most of the smaller and incredibly affordable meals will come with beans, soup, a side salad, tortillas, and rice. The grilled pork or pork fajitas, for example, will come with all the sides and cost you the equivalent of $4–5 US. Larger plates, including a marvelous grilled chicken breast stuffed with ham and cheese, or the fish fillet of the day cooked in butter, with a creamy sauce of some kind, tomatoes, onions, and peppers, will arrive at your table with rice, beans, a salad, guacamole, and chips. The amount of food you get here per your order is simply staggering.

For larger groups, share one of the Tampiquenas (grilled meat or fish with a variety of sides). Options include plates with several samples of seafood, pork, fajita, chicken, or any of the above together which will easily feed four and are beyond inexpensive. Clean with plenty of available seating and a short 10-minute walk from town.

Phone: 52-987-872-1295
(Corner of calle 3 and 25)

A & D Modern Pub $$

This phenomenal little spot could have been in the last section, but regardless, A & D is such a welcome island addition, it is difficult to know where to begin with this fun place! Part café, part bistro, and part urban pub, with a menu filled with items that are all like the resoundingly successful result of some crazy culinary adventure! In their own words, "If it's not messy, it's not A & D Kitchen."

The menu is continually evolving, with weekly changes, and creative twists. Sandwiches and burgers are king here, along with a perfect brisket and their own smoked and pulled pork. A smoked chicken sandwich with rosemary smoked mushrooms, and Swiss cheese dripping from the sides, garnished with a toothpick on top with cheese and grape tomatoes, or the pastrami sandwich on a pretzel bun, or the spicy peanut butter bacon smash burger, oozing with juices and hot cheese! Everything is served with fries or a house salad, and either the house coleslaw or their Cajun-style pasta salad. I'm sorry, but have I even discussed the desserts here, or the hand-crafted cocktails, delicious margaritas and mojitos? I have not, but they are as creative and imaginative as the food.

One of the best new spots on the island for lunch and dinner, a staff as sweet as they come, and a place where, Montreal, Canadian and tastes of the world combine with astounding results! A & D is way fun!
Phone: 52-984-253-9365
(On 10, between 2 & 4)

Cuatro Tacos $$$

This isn't a small family spot, it is actually owned and operated by a group of island investors responsible for some wonderful and fancier restaurants (Kinta and Kondessa are 2 of them), but Cuatro Tacos is small and serves great tacos from a limited menu. These are nothing like the street and more affordable choices at some of the places I have mentioned in this section though, Cuatro Tacos are more "designer" tacos and not cheap, but they are excellent if you are in the mood for something a bit different.

First off, the selection of margaritas is good and range from the classic most of us are familiar with, to a Mezcal margarita with just a hint of smokey Mezcal flavor. The tacos of which there is a selection of 8, not to mention the Lobster Tacos, include a chicken breast with mole, to a stuffed chile with chihuahua cheese, are served in a variety of tortilla styles from yellow corn, to blue corn tortillas, even a green cactus tortilla. If you aren't in the mood for tacos, stick with their excellent fajitas. They have a sampler plate for two which includes all the tacos, less the lobster.
Phone: 52-987-800-8809
(Calle 3 between Melgar and 5)

Los Arcos $

Back to the more standard and authentic island recipes with the fun, Taqueria Los Arcos. Pretty much as basic as basic can be. An assortment of tacos and tortas with familiar choices from cheese, chorizo (sausage), smoked pork, chicken, and a few others. They have been on the island a long time and they have quite the following, including me. An assortment of filled burritos is also available, as well as agua frescas, soda, but no alcohol. The salsa sides are a variety of very hot to mild, be sure to ask. Opens late morning depending on the season and will typically close by 6:00 p.m.
Phone: 52-987-119-8121
(Ave. 30, between 5 & 7)

Taqueria Diaz 100% $

One last classically authentic pure Cozumel taqueria along the ever-popular local evening dining destination, the lively Avenida 30. This boulevard divided street buzzes night and day, but evenings are when all the local families come out after 6ish and dine at the tremendous number of little establishments up and down this long stretch. Taqueria Diaz moved across the street to the west side of Ave. 30, but nothing has changed.

Their amazing selection of tacos are nearly all under the equivalent of $1.00 US, and for some reason a bit more filling than others. Nothing fancy, but very clean, always friendly and while little English is spoken, it is very easy to navigate the menu items as most are in Spanish and English. As with all local taquerias, their take on salsas is a little different than the rest, with the usual combination of hot and mild. The pastor pork is slightly caramelized once cooked, giving it a sweet and unique taste compared to others, it is divine. Beer is available.

Phone: 52-987-116-2069

(Ave. 30, between 2 & 4)

Caribe Burger $

What a fun little spot just a block or so off the square with simple and excellent food. You may have guessed they have burgers, and yes, they do! Not only juicy burgers, but some of the best onion rings I've ever had, homemade and not frozen, and the burritos are a treat too! Seriously, for a burger fix on Cozumel, the creations of those at Caribe Burger are well worth the visit.

Phone: 52-987-872-3580

(Just west of 5 on Salas)

El Pescador $$

On the remote east side of the island, this little restaurant is part of a larger sort of beach club with beautiful sand, hammocks, and facilities for a full day on the beach, including being the home of Cozumel Surfing, which will be discussed later. El Pescador will open around 10:30 a.m. like all the others on this side, and they will close by 5–6ish daily. This side of the island has no electricity and rarely if ever cell phone service until you reach the transversal road on the north end of the east side road.

The reason I include El Pescador in this section is their marvelous large platter of mixed ceviche which is possibly the best I have ever had. I have shared a plate with 6 of us and we did not finish what we were served. They have a full menu of assorted island dishes from sandwiches, to tacos, fajitas, grilled fish, and much more, but this ceviche is special.

Phone: 52-987-872-7440

(East side of the island maybe 2 miles south of the transversal road, you can't miss it)

La Classica $$

I would be remiss if I didn't mention the delicious modern take on the street taco at La Classica Restaurant. I am a little nervous going against my history of keeping "new" places out of the books for a couple of years at least, but this place is backed well, the food is yummy and I think it will be here for a long time to come.

Mentioned earlier under dinners, it deserves mention again as an innovative and unique presentation of typical Mexican cuisine which sets this place apart for new twists on tacos and tostadas, not to mention the shrimp enchiladas. Very affordable for something so exemplary.

(On 5, between 4 & 6)

El Sazón Del Camaron $

I don't rate these in any order of significance, though this place east of town is simply marvelous. Right on the busy Ave. Benito Juarez as you head out of town on the way to the other side, stop in for some of the island's best eats. Either visit on your way to shop at the new Chedraui, or maybe on your way out to the east side of the island, but if you plan on stopping here on your way back from the east side, they close at 3:30 p.m. You will be joining a lot of locals here, either in the fairly large indoor seating area or outdoors along the street where you will find 5–6 tables.

Local recipes are used for their authentic tortas, tacos, ceviches, and seafood plates. Four different sauces come with your meal, two are really hot, one is a mild pico de gallo, and some kind of chipotle that is heavenly. Fried fish and shrimp, the mixed ceviche (I ask for no octopus, for so many reasons I just won't eat it) feeds at least 4, and the garlic chicken or shrimp tacos and breaded shrimp tortas are my go-to.

Phone: 52-987-120-4664
(Ave. Juarez on the corner with 55)

Arabian Tacos $

What a special little place. I wish I could say I have tried Arabian Tacos more than once, but I haven't, though I sampled as much as I could! I think technically it is Lebanese, but whatever, and it is FAR more than just tacos for sure. I had the hummus which was creamily astounding and 3 chicken tacos (with some sort of awesome cheese), plus a bowl of the lentil soup since I was getting a cold. I asked for just a taste of the natural yogurt, they obliged, and it was wonderful as were the brownies that I ordered and took home with me for a late-night snack. Just a small taste of this fun place was an array of delights, spice, and flavor, I cannot wait to return.

Arabian coffee, falafel, lemonade with mint, tabbouleh, fresh bread, homemade cookies, and other desserts, and a menu filled with treats of middle eastern inspiration. I don't believe there is anything else like it on the island.

There are 6 tables under a spreading outdoor grape vine-covered patio to keep you in the shade, and a few tables indoors. Hours, depending on the season, are 11:30 a.m.–11:30 p.m. For what you get here, this is a bargain on Cozumel serving something you just might not expect.

Phone: 52-987-120-8282
(Ave. 30 between 2 & 4)

K'ooben Laab $

Very, very different, simple, and elegant artisanal food in one. Pasta aficionados rave about the homemade pastas here, as well as the sophisticated desserts from a chocolate cake that is above and beyond, to a large selection of which I couldn't tell you what it is, but the few I've had were amazing.

You might not expect much as you pass by, but if it is homemade Italian you crave, the word on the street is K'ooben Laab! Recently with the addition of an upstairs terrace, they have expanded their small space. Freshly baked breads including olive bread, cheese bread, and others, inspired Italian sauces, to a fairly impressive wine selection for such a small spot. K'ooben Laab is part bakery, part restaurant, and part dessert destination. This is a place as different as nearly any on the island, serving up pure excellence as a bakery, restaurant, and dessert heaven! Incredibly affordable.

Phone: 52-987-100-4726
(Ave. 3, between Jose Maria Morelos and 5)

Ernestos Fajita Factory $$

I have been visiting Ernestos for many years while coming to the island, this is an island institution on the south end as you drive out of town. Near the last cruise ship piers and next to the Atlantis Submarine, just look for the orange building and his rental vehicles out front, about 3 miles south of the Playa ferry pier.

Breakfast, lunch, and dinner are served, but as the name says, it is the fajitas, well, and I think the nachos are pretty stellar as well, also the key lime pie! This is a great family place, share the array of fajitas and nachos, and folks can indulge in a very good margarita, there are several options. The shrimp fajitas are my favorite. The views are beautiful with lots of boat activity, BIG ships, but regardless, sit out on the deck if you can.

Phone: 52-987-872-3152
(On the main road about 3 miles south of the Playa ferry pier)

GREAT PIZZAS

I have discussed pizzas a bit in the dining section and while everyone's tastes are different, it is tough to go wrong with any of these. Great pizza is all about the seasoned sauce, crust, and the freshness of the ingredients. All of these are a bit different and excellent for the pizza connoisseur.

Guidos $$

Amazing pizzas with perfect crusts, just a tad crispy and sensational. Most are with mozzarella, and while I am not a vegetarian by any means, I am a meat lover, but rarely here. The Vegetarian White Pizza, or the Swiss White are divine for one or two, or the Margherita with mozzarella, slices of tomato, and a perfect sauce, with basil. Enjoy one of the island's loveliest atmospheres and the most renowned pizzas.

Phone: 52-987-872-0946
(Rafael Melgar, between 6 & 8)

New Especias $$

This popular Italian restaurant has 12 or so pizzas on the menu along with their other Italian delights. The Fresh Tomato with slices of tomatoes you might imagine, basil and oregano, slathered with mozzarella, or the 4 Cheese Pizza is delectably blended with mozzarella, Parmesan, provolone, and gorgonzola, or the classic pepperoni, and for seafood lovers try the lobster or shrimp pizzas. A special treat.

Phone: 52-987-869-7947
(Ohn calle 3, between 5 & 10)

Ohana $$

I think it is the only Chicago Deep Dish pizza on the island, so enjoy it in a quiet neighborhood with a pleasant setting in their outdoor back garden. Not a tough crust like so many I have had in the states, this crust and pizza is perfectly excellent. Unique, so friendly, and fun.

(On 5, between 6 & 8)

Cerveceria Punta Sur $$

Pizza and great beer, just like it is supposed to be at Cozumel's first microbrewery. This is a casual pizza stop with excellent choices in pizza and beer, not pretentious whatsoever, only a pleasant and laid-back atmosphere with excellent wood-fired pizzas, select ales, and smiles. The Lionfish Pizza (lionfish is an invasive fish from the local reefs, however lionfish are quite tasty), is a delicious pizza, probably the most popular here. I lean toward the Hawaiian Pizza and an amber beer. They are a proud supporter of local artists as well as an innovative and very fun stop on the island.

(On 10, between Salas and 3)

Sorrisi

This is romantic, with delicious Italian food and pizzas just off the main drag in town. A bit more expensive than the others here, but for the authentic pizza lover looking for something from the streets of maybe Taranto, Italy, this may be your closest bet. They also have a very good wine selection.

Phone: 52-987-869-0960

(On calle 3, between Rafael Melgar and 5)

"When you cease to make a contribution, you begin to die."

Eleanor Roosevelt

ROMANTIC SETTINGS

So, romance is in the eye of the romantic and we are all different. Whether it's a quiet corner and dim lights or a view for the ages, or maybe candlelight and a bottle of wine, these are a few that should fit the bill. It is always a good idea to scope a table or location out ahead of time and make a reservation if the night is a truly special one.

La Monina $$

Begin your evening at La Monina with a stroll down the Malecon before settling in for your dinner, take in the views, then walk up the steps into this palapa covered, open-air restaurant looking out over the water. With a glass of sangria, you can watch the sunset over the distant Yucatan jungles, and the boats coming in. The bistro lights strung throughout help create an enchanting ambiance after dark. Share one of the large choice salads, or one of their grilled fresh choices from the sea. The wine list isn't much though it is adequate, the margaritas are excellent, as is the sangria. They will tone down any music they are playing if you request. I have requested this at lunch and they happily obliged. They typically won't have loud music here, especially after dark.

Phone: 52-987-872-5762

(About a 10-minute walk north from the ferry pier to Playa, you can't miss the 3 large palapas)

Guidos $$

If you arrive here early enough, grab one of the few tables along the sidewalk, share one of their many good bottles of wine, or a glass of their famous sangria, and take in a sunset. From there, enter the doors and begin an evening of what may be the essence of romantic dining in Cozumel. Funky lanterns hanging from the branches of a large tree and tropical foliage create a dreamy landscape after dark. Delectable and beautifully arranged salads, exquisitely presented and prepared Italian specialties, and pizzas which the team here have been creating for years. Finish your evening with a Crème Brulee, one of their ice creams, or any number of many desserts as artistically crafted as anything else in this Cozumel treasure.

Phone: 52-987-872-0946

(Rafael Melgar, between 6 & 8)

La Chardonnay $$

Possibly the most underrated restaurant on the island, yet those who have taken the time to dine here ALWAYS rave about it. You will cherish the tropical vibe after dark, the subtly lit intimate lush gardens in back, and the consistent wonderfully cheerful service. Seating is available either out front on the porch, indoors, or in the open-air garden in the back. In a quiet neighborhood far from the buzz of downtown, yet only a short walk from the square, romance awaits you here after dark.

The pink paint and palapa roof is hard to miss, as this cute little building stands out on the back streets of San Miguel. I love the front porch where only 2 small tables await you, and if you are here for a romantic evening, they will gladly bring a candle to your table. La Chardonnay is on a quiet corner in town, and while there is a small convenience store across the street, it only adds to the fun of viewing local life as it really is on Cozumel. Pizza, pastas, seafood, steaks, crisp generous salads, and Yucatecan recipes dating back centuries fill the large menu. Find your way to this remarkable little island gem.

Phone: 52 987 872 1351

(On the corner of 7 & 5, a short walk south from the square)

Kondessa $$$

Just down the street from Chardonnay, Kondessa awaits you with charm, elegance, and culinary delights. A bit more expensive than others, as the food here is a gallery of gourmet twists on historic Mexican recipes. They offer a couples dining experience per their website, I am not sure what that entails, but Kondessa knows their craft well and I can assure you it would be a special experience.

Lots of different cocktails, margaritas, and the wine list is better than most. After dark, the atmosphere softens to one of magical serene beauty with a variety of funky lanterns hanging from branches, accented and colorful base lit walls, and an atmosphere well worth a special night out for two. Share the Lobster Enchiladas, and be sure to try their guacamole samples (I think there are 4), they are different and amazing. If you prefer traditional guacamole, they will accommodate you definitely, but I encourage you to expand your horizons if you love guacamole.

Finish a beautiful evening at Kondessa with an array of desserts, including their ever-popular Coconut ice cream.
Phone: 52-987-869-1086
(Ave, 5, between 5 & 7)

The Lobster House $$

I include this charming location because here you will experience the history and lore of Cozumel dining dating back decades. The family's Lobster House and the sons, Fernando's Lobster House, are directly next door to each other, and they represent what this island is all about with traditional seafood, particularly hand-selected lobster, in a simple after dark location north of town.

Far from much else on the island, have a cab drop you here after 7:00 p.m. and you can enjoy an ambiance that is purely old-world Cozumel. Roughly two miles north of town in the quiet northern hotel district, an evening here is romantic, and it is where you will enjoy lobster of any size you wish, selected by you, and prepared by those who have specialized in the art of lobster for many years.

Lush and beautiful, this family operation invites you to join them for a unique and pleasant evening in Cozumel. The Key Lime Pie has proven so popular there is a separate location directly next door (The Key Lime Pie Factory) where you can come and try the dessert without a meal, or you are more than welcome to finish your meal with this amazing pie in either restaurant.
Phone: 52-987-107-3116
(Across from the Westin in the northern hotel zone)

Others on the island where a romantic setting awaits you.

- **Sorrisi, La Chef**
- **Pepe's**
- **Shii Fu**
- **Buccanos**
- **La Cocay**
- **Panchos Backyard**
- **El Palomar**
- **Casa Mission**

SEAFOOD

You will find sensationally prepared seafood all over Cozumel, from the most elegant, to the simplest, but some set the standard. I encourage you to interact and talk with other travelers, you will learn a lot, and never be afraid to try something new. Have fun with these suggestions, you will not go wrong.

Pescaderia San Carlos $

A combination of a fresh fish market where locals and other restaurants come to purchase their fish daily, and a small restaurant serving the same fresh fish, adds up to one of the island's best locations to dine on traditionally prepared seafood. Fillets, pan-fried whole fish, ceviches, shrimp, lobster, and much more are all served at San Carlos, and those in the know flock here to one of the islands most well-known, and affordable seafood establishments.
(Calle 3 and biz 55)

La Choza $

Just a block or so away from the town square, La Choza has been satisfying the seafood urges of locals, travelers, and expats for decades. Traditional family recipes carefully prepared with years of experience and an understanding of what makes a superb meal from the freshest local fish. Dine on excellent local seafood recipes with a tasty margarita.

Phone: 52-987-872-0958

(On 10, between A.R. Salas and 3 sur)

El Pescador $$

I know many of you have visited here for a day on the beach, one of the east side's best beach bars, but have you tried the food? A friend turned me on to the mixed ceviche platter which easily fed 5–6 of us, it was amazing. Something like $20.00 US, it was packed with bits and pieces of fish, conch, and whatever else was available that day. The fish and shrimp tacos are delicious as are the fish fillets, lightly breaded or pan-fried in butter, with just the right spices used to complement the natural flavor. You will find other fabulous recipes and seafood on this remote side of the island during the day, but during my last 2 visits, this became a stop for the ceviche. The east side is only open from 10:00 a.m. daily until usually 5:00–6:00 p.m., as there is no electricity and all the spots close for the night and return in the morning.

Phone: 52-987-872-7440

(About 2 miles south of where the transversal road meets the east side)

La Perlita $$

Sensational in a simple way, these are local folks who know how to select and prepare the best seafood. If you are a seafood or fish lover, La Perlita needs to be a must-visit on Cozumel. Great margaritas and a nearly limitless number of choices whether it is on the menu or not, they will prepare per your request. Stuffed lobster, a lightly and perfectly seasoned breading on the fillets, and a grilled lobster which was a first for me anywhere.

Phone: 52-987-869-8343

(Ave. 65 & 10)

Buccanos $$$

This trendy and popular outstanding restaurant seems to be able to do little wrong. They have taken this island by storm and the meals are different takes on tradition, exquisite and impeccably prepared and presented. The seafood is no exception, and while it is not a seafood restaurant, what they do offer is supposed to be amazing. The lobster is prepared in a couple of ways and part of different dishes. They offer a Seafood Risotto and a mixed seafood sort of shish kebab (skewer). For seafood in a bit more of an elegant setting, Buccanos is a very fine choice.

Phone: 044-987-114-5607

(A mile or so north of town in the northern hotel zone)

**A handful of other can't miss choices on the island, enjoy!

- **El Palomar**
- **Azul Madera**
- **Casa Dennis**
- **Blue Angel**
- **El Moro**
- **La Conchita Del Caribe**
- **Los Morros Del Morrito**
- **El Sazon Del Camaron**
- **Casa Mission**
- **The Lobster House**

CHOICE STEAKS

It was not long ago that finding a fine steak, properly prepared, was a very difficult task on this island. While it is still not remotely Kansas City, the availability of select meats has improved in the past 10 years, and there are several restaurants where a good steak is a reality. I am not by any means a steak aficionado and have never had a steak while visiting the island.

La Cocay $$

This place is like the "little engine that could," and it can. Quietly, just as the neighborhood it is in, La Cocay continues to impress all who dine there. The skirt steak is a common item on the menu, and while it is a cut not known for its tender nature, skirt steak IS renowned for its flavor. La Cocay does a superb job with their steak options, as they do in their kitchen with all the Italian and Mexican choices on the menu of what is easily a top ten restaurant in Cozumel.

Phone: 52-987-872-5533
(On calle 8, between 10 & 15)

Pepe's $$$

For many years now, Pepe's has sort of been one of the go-to options for those in search of a special Cozumel dining experience, and one of the few homes of a choice steak. Their menu offers Rib Eyes and New York Strips.

Phone: 52-987-872-0213
(Rafael Melgar near the corner of A. R. Salas)

Del Sur Argentina $$

This is another Cozumel restaurant I have never tried; it just seems like they are always closed from the looks of it outside. That could not be further from the truth from what I understand. Best known for an array of remarkable empanadas filled with an assortment of meats, potatoes, and veggies. Apparently their Argentine meats will cure your appetite for a good steak, in particular the Rib Eyes and Flank steaks. All with an assortment of dessert items,

Phone: 52-987-871-5744
(NE corner of 3 & 5)

Azul Madera $$$

Another apparent home to some delicious steaks is the cosmopolitan-style, smartly detailed, and inventive local restaurant Azul Madera. If the Filet Mignon and New York Angus Steak are anything like the rest of their menu items, I am sure they are prepared to perfection.

Phone: 52-987-872-2708
(On 3, between 5 & 10)

RESTAURANTS IF YOUR KIDS NEED A TASTE OF HOME

Nothing is really wrong with an urge for home when on the island, and it isn't just kids that may want a taste of home when traveling. I don't mean to exclude any nationalities, but this small section is mostly for kids and those with tastes leaning north, who may want to indulge in some of the more common US foods you will find on the island.

Hooters $$

Chicken breast strips, hamburger sliders, onion rings, cheese sticks, Hooters burgers, a variety of chicken wings with all the sauces, and a buffalo chicken sandwich all should at least temporarily curb your desires, otherwise, get out and try the wonderful local fare and all the international cuisine this island offers.

Phone: 52-987-869-1465

(Part of the Punta Langosta Cruise ship complex just south of town)

Palmeras $$

Breakfast, lunch, and dinner and a little bit of everything on the menu, though all a bit refined for the crowds. Palmeras has been here forever, and it was the first place most people saw on the island for many years until the cruise ships arrived. If you crave Mexican you will certainly find it here, if you crave tastes from up north you will find them too, Palmeras tries to have a little something for everyone. Bacon and egg breakfast with everything from hash browns, to pancakes and syrup, poached eggs, a club sandwich, chicken sandwiches, burgers, good ribs and so much more.

Phone: 52-987-872-0532

(Right at the ferry pier to Playa Del Carmen)

Rock 'N Java $$

Rock 'N Java is so good and so welcoming to any who pass through their doors. By no means are they limited whatsoever to the menu items of this section, Rock 'N Java has food across the board from delicious seafood to pasta, Mexican cuisine and much more, but their gringo food, even with a small kid's menu is wonderful. Chili cheese fries, French fries, chicken tenders, excellent burgers, a BLT, a Turkey, Chicken and Bacon Club, and for the little one's menu, spaghetti, chicken tenders, French fries, and pancakes.

Their desserts will please anyone! Banana Nut Cake, Chocolate Cheesecake, Brownies, Apple Pie, Carrot Cake, and a few more sweet tooth options!

Phone: 52-987-872-4405

(Just south of the Punta Langosta cruise ship pier)

Jeanie's Waffle House $$

Like the above ONLY in that they serve wonderful food across genres, all 3 have been long-standing good stewards of the island and serve food from Mexican to gringo land. Jeanie's serves breakfast, lunch, and dinner and provides those leaning north with wonderful options. Two eggs with ham or bacon, cooked any way you would like, Eggs Benedict that is out of this world, all the waffles they offer like the Chocolate Chip Waffles, French Toast, a Reuben sandwich, BLT and a bacon cheeseburger to name a few. The kid's menu has hot dogs and grilled cheese, both with fries.

Phone: 52-987-878-4647

(Just south of the Punta Langosta cruise ship pier)

Kelley's Sports Bar & Grill $$

Not only is Kelley's one of the most fun places to watch your NFL games, especially if you are a Packer fan, but the food for the US spoiled football fan is pretty sweet too. Mouthwatering ribs, chicken wings, great burgers, and a Reuben sandwich if you are so inclined. They have lots more good eats here but come and find out for yourself at this local Cozumel sports bar.

Phone: 52-987-878-4738

(Ave. 10, between Salas and 1)

Dick's Dive $$

A very cool outdoor vibe on the pedestrian walk just south of the town square and the 7 Eleven (yes there is a 7 Eleven). Dick's always has a cheerful staff and fun food for nearly anyone, with a good local menu, some pastas, and a few treats for those that want a little extra. The Bacon Cheeseburger, Western Burger and Guacamole Burger, all served with fries are wonderful, I have had all three! Onion rings, shrimp and bacon tacos, and both shrimp or chicken jalapeno poppers, excellent! Good sports venue on television except they don't like to turn the music down if you really want to listen to your game.

(Just south of the town square on the pedestrian walk)

The Money Bar and Beach Club $$

South of town a bit, with a large covering palapa, a very large seating area, plenty of parking, and a somewhat mellow beach club environment, The Money Bar is a great place for a sunset, large groups, and some gringo food. Don't get me wrong, they have much more on their menu, a very good wine and champagne selection, and consistently good food.

The menu includes bagel sandwiches, a selection of chicken wings, darn good burgers, a big hot dog, club sandwiches, and a BLT. The Money Bar has a fun kid's menu if they must have a hot dog or grilled cheese. Bring the whole family here for a sunset.

Phone: 52-987-869-5140

(Maybe 2 miles south of the last cruise ship pier along the old road)

Woody's Bar & Grill $$

Gather up a table along the pedestrian walk with your family and friends at this iconic stop with daily hours of operation from 9:30 a.m.-midnight (depending on the season), and 10:00–2:00 a.m. Saturdays. Just off the square, and a block east of the ferry pier from the mainland, Woody's has a host of menu items from delicious seafood, to Mexican, and a good number of items if you are a bit tired of the local fare. This is the closest thing to a hoppin' summer Midwest bar on Cozumel. If that is what you are looking for. Even if you are not, Woody's is a lot of fun.

Hot or mild Chicken Wings with sauces including Thousand Island, sour cream, honey mustard, ranch, and blue cheese. They also have spaghetti with garlic bread, tender ribs, and mashed potatoes with coleslaw and pork 'n beans, grilled cheese, chili dogs, and excellent burgers. Live music all day, every day.

(Along the pedestrian walk on the northeast corner of the square)

LOCAL HAMBUERGESAS AND STREET FOOD STANDS

The food carts and street food stands will move around often, but if you visit the town square (Parque Benito Juarez) by the ferry pier at night, or walk along Avenida 30 (J. Coldwell), maybe a 6 block walk east from the square, you will find a lot of them. On Ave. 30, start about Calle 8 and walk south, you will find tons of local treats in the next 10 blocks or so.

FOR THE VEGETARIAN

Most dining establishments on the island have some sort of vegetarian options, whether a salad or whatever, but I suppose it depends on your level of vegetarian. If you are vegan, I have no idea really, but I do believe you are in good hands on the island. I will note a few below that are well-known vegetarian options, though since I am not one, I will refrain from too much comment.

Arabian Tacos $

Excellent in every way. Tahini, falafels, hummus, and lots of other fun and vegetarian-friendly menu items that will serve the vegetarian well.

Phone: 52-987-120-8282

(Ave. 30, between 2 & 4)

K'ooben Laab $

Vegan, and plenty of vegetarian options with pastas, salads, vegetables with everything, fresh homemade breads, and delicious desserts. I hope being a vegan doesn't mean you can't enjoy the desserts here; they are a sweet tooth's dream.

Phone: 52-987-100-4726

(Ave. 30, between Morelos and 5)

Cali Café $

I am not remotely a vegan, but this little inspired and delicious café touts itself as all vegan, but I challenge you to not love each dish you try here! Stacked burgers, French Toast, omelets, burritos, and wraps, especially the Thai Wrap was awesome. The selection of smoothies and freshly squeezed juices, not to mention their desserts, like the chocolate and carrot cakes, and oh yes, a Key Lime Pie (my favorite) with an avocado base, wow, very different but so good.

Indoors, has AC and they have added a new outdoor terrace area. This place is steaming ahead in popularity for very good reason. Breakfast, lunch, and dinner typically and prices are very reasonable.

Phone: 52-987-872-6275

(A.R. Salas, between 10 & 15)

Colores Y Sabores $

I have not been, but I will as the word is out this place is pure farm to table excellent Mexican food. The owner is sweet as can be and serves up her delectable takes on traditional recipes. Soups, tacos, enchiladas, fajitas, and the guacamole are supposed to be divine. Of course, the margaritas and beer will get me there too. This will be my first stop next visit. Vegetarian friendly.

(Just off the main drag on calle 5)

BEST GUACAMOLE

This is one of those sections where you might say, "Isn't everywhere good, we are in Mexico?" Surprisingly yes, the guacamole is good at nearly every stop you will make, but the following are consistently traditional, always delicious, all a tad different and all sampled by me. I love my guacamole almost as much as a properly made margarita! So often, great guacamole comes down to the little things. The quality and consistency of the avocado, the freshness of the tomatoes (if used), is it made with cilantro or not, how much salt (too much, or too little are common mistakes), are the chips fresh (this is hugely important), or is a touch of cumin added? The big one is, how long ago was it prepared. Enjoy your sampling, if you are a guacamole connoisseur, search any of these out!

*While this list may seem a tad redundant, please, please keep in mind, that every one of these Cozumel establishments has worked diligently to earn their respect in the community, and ALL are a reflection of why we all come here in the first place.

La Choza $

Everything about La Choza is traditionally excellent, including their guacamole and chips.

Phone: 52-987-872-0958

(On 10, between A.R. Salas and 3 sur)

Kondesa Cozumel $$

The traditional guacamole at this elegant and quirky island restaurant is simply sensational. They have a couple of other options of guac that are supposed to be sensational, but I always stick to traditional. Late afternoon or early evening, sit at the small bar, enjoy one of their great cocktails, and some magnificent guacamole. You will most likely want to stay for dinner!

Phone: 52-987-869-1086

(On 5, between 5 & 7)

Casa Denis $

The longest standing restaurant on the island has been creating this highlight of Mexican cuisine for decades. It is as you would expect, nearly perfect.

Phone: 52-987-872-0067

(On the southeast pedestrian walk of the town square)

Taqueria Rafas $

Please find yourself at this quintessential tiny Cozumel family-run cantina at least once during your visit, as everything including the guacamole is superb.

(Calle 10, between 15 & 20)

Casa Mission $$

You will want to visit this beautiful restaurant for many reasons. Traditionally elegant with many, many years of old family recipes, including their guacamole.

Phone: 52-987-872-1641

(Corner of Ave. 55 with Benito Juarez)

Señor Iguanas $

One of the oldest little spots on the east side of the island with creamy delicious guacamole, and crisp fresh chips.

Phone: 52-987-105-6344

(Just south of the transversal road)

Mezcalito's $

Excellent guacamole will greet you here, as will nearly everything on the menu of one of the east side's most well-known beach bars. Play the ring game!

Phone: 52-987-876-0914

(Right where the transversal road meets the east side of the island)

Las Palmas $

Simple and nearly perfect at this local spot.

Phone: 52-987-872-1295

(Calle 3 & 25)

Los Tacotales (Formerly Los Otates) $

Delicious local and authentic everything, but the chips are always thick and crisp, and the guacamole is fresh.
Phone: 52-987-120-1076
(Ave. 15, between A. R. Salas and 3 sur)

Los Arcos $

It's the little things that make everything at Los Arcos a must stop for anyone in search of traditional Mexican street food.
Phone: 52-987-119-8121
(Ave. 30, between 5 & 7)

Chilangos $

As with so many of these small taquerias along Ave. 30, the locals flock to them in the evenings for dining in or carry-out. Chilangos guacamole is a local favorite.
Phone: 52-987-872-3072
(Ave. 30, just south of 3)

Diego's Tacos $

Every item here is prepared with you in mind, and with the loving touch of this remarkable family that has made such an impact on travelers to Cozumel. I for one, make Diego's a first and last stop each visit to the island.
Phone: 52-987-564-9802
(Right across from the airport under the red tent)

La Conchita Del Caribe $

Amazing everything from fresh seafood to delicious guacamole. A local favorite.
Phone: 52-987-869-1218
(Ave. 65, between 13 & 15)

*Others that serve the guacamole world well!

- **Pescaderia San Carlos**
- **El Rincon De Addy**
- **El Palomar**
- **The Lobster House (es)**
- **Playa Corona**
- **La Cocina De Silvia**
- **El Pescador**
- **El Moro**
- **Rock 'N Java**
- **Buccanos**
- **Los Moros Del Morrito**
- **Panchos Backyard**
- **El Sazon De Camaron**
- **La Perlita**
- **The Liquor Box**

" If you reject the food, ignore the customs, fear the religion and avoid the people, you might better stay at home."

James Michener

BAKERIES, AND A FINE CHOCOLATE SHOP

Baked goods, pastries, and fresh breads are seemingly taking over at all restaurants, the options are exploding daily. While this section will focus primarily on bakeries, most of them, if not all, act as something else on the island. The large grocery stores of Cozumel

(Mega, Chedraui, Super Aki) also prepare and sell some excellent breads and pastries, don't forget them.

Zermatt Bakery $

Located in this same spot for as long as I can remember, Zermatt consistently bakes some of the tastiest treats on Cozumel. They have delicious hot muffins, fresh breads, ham and cheese pastry sandwiches, and much more. Enjoy a quiet morning outside on the front porch at one of the 4–5 tables with a cup of coffee and plan your day. Don't even think of smoking, they do not like it.

Mentioned earlier under our breakfast section, one could make a meal out of the sweets here each morning, the products are very, very good. Check out the pigeons daily as they congregate on the corner with crumbs tossed out by the bakery, they are in heaven. Seriously though, tiny cream cheese pies, cinnamon rolls, cookies, fudge brownies, and fresh cheese-filled Danish, Zermatt is incredible.

(On the corner of 4 & 5, just north of the square)

El Coffee $

El Coffee is both a breakfast place (as mentioned earlier) and a bakery. Coffees, lattes and such for the caffeine fix, and treats for any time of day. Sponge cakes, coffee cakes, apple pies, even full cakes (order one if you want), banana breads, pastries, cheesecakes, cookies, even a good peanut butter pie. Most everything is available whole or by the slice. El Coffee rocks!

Phone: 52-987-869-0456

(In town on calle 3, between Rafael Melgar and 5)

The Maple Bakehouse $

With two locations in town now, the delicious treats at Maple Bakehouse are sensational. I discussed their breakfasts and baked goods a bit earlier, but my lord, the bakers, and their recipes here are artists. Honey, Nutella, chocolate and more crazy croissants, different homemade breads, from Multi-Grain, to cheese bread, to a bread filled with cream cheese! Different cheesecakes and cinnamon buns, as well as a wide assortment of fresh pastries. Very tough to pass up. Have fun!

Phone: 52-987-869-2418

(Corner of 6 & 5 in town, or on Ave. 30, between 17 & 19)

La Panaderia Cozumelena

Right next door to the east from Restaurant La Cozumelena, the traditional Mexican bakery is simple and wonderful with everything made fresh and on-site. They offer a delightful array of breads, sweet rolls, and even donuts.

Phone: 52-987-869-0213

(Ave. 10 sur, and calle 3 sur)

Panaderia y Pasteleria San Martin de Porres $

A delicious and locally owned little bakery maybe a 10-minute walk east of town with fresh breads, pastries, muffins, fruit turnovers, and lots of other daily treats of which I had no idea. I had a flat tire right in front of this place on a morning research ride and the darling lady in the shop commiserated with me by offering me something from the selection. I bought some sort of cheese bread and she wrapped up a couple of fruit empanadas of some kind that were warm and just outstanding. I made a point of stopping here several times my last trip. It is so charming and filled with aromas and smiles.

Phone: 52-987-872-5701
(Ave. 30, just south of 5)

Genesis Tortilleria $

Not a bakery, just fresher than fresh tortillas made on-site. They do offer some other items, but I forget. Tiny and dedicated to tortillas that are picked up by locals and restaurants all morning. I've walked in just wanting to buy 10 and they smile and just give them to me.

(Calle 6, between 25 & 30)

Mary's Tortilleria $

Same as above, just a simple tortilla factory, baked fresh and serving them up by weight daily until about 1:00 p.m.

(On 10, between 4 & 6)

Neysi Pasteleria

Cakes to order, or in stock, cupcakes, cookies, and other various baked goods. This is a tiny spot and they are so friendly.

Phone: 52-987-872-3810
(Southwest corner of 30 and 3 sur)

Fervic Pasteleria

Not sure if this is owned by (Neysi above, or vice versa) or what, but they are close to each other. They are both tiny and excellent and will bend over to any request you have. I love these two small bakeries! They will design AND deliver cakes per request for birthdays, anniversaries, weddings and any occasion, and they serve by the slice.

Phone: 52-987-872-7583
(Just north of the corner of 30 and 3, on 30)

Chocolateria Isla Bella $$$

An artisanal chocolate manufacturer right here on Cozumel? Yes, there is. The mother and daughter that have operated this delightful little shop for nearly 10 years are true food artisans, they have become masters at their craft. From their handsomely designed packaging to the shop layout and aromas which will capture your senses and not let them go once you enter the doors; the products and presentation here have been carefully thought out with outstanding results.

All the products are made on sight and while I know they have worked hard to try and grow some of their own cacao locally, that is an entirely different task than creating the finish product masterpieces they do here. So, sourcing the natural cacao for this operation is an ongoing search I would assume. Everything is available via their website or of course here in Cozumel.

They may be a little heavy on the dark chocolates, but it's never bothered me, and if they are not too busy, ask for a brief tour and learn the fascinating and arduous process that takes place here daily. Then be sure to buy something from their wonderful display and select choices. Bags and bars of Mexican sipping chocolate, sea salt chocolates, white chocolate, dark chocolates, toffees, bonbons, caramels, truffles, and the "Bean to Bar" chocolate bar, as they call it, yum. Various nuts, lime, different subtly used peppers, and other products, are used in the creation of Cozumel's best chocolates at Isla Bella.

Phone: 52-987-111-8462

(On 5, between 2 & 4, just north of the square)

Patio Cakes and Desserts $$

An artist with cakes, cupcakes, cookies, and more, Kathy is quickly becoming somewhat legendary with her theme-based cakes. She doesn't really operate a storefront, but her work is available through Facebook. I hesitate to even include this here, but I have heard such good things about the work and her delicious and beautiful cakes.

(@patiocakes, or +52 987 869 2004)

GREAT SMOOTHIES

I'm not going into any depth here, but some of us just love a fruit smoothie on a hot tropical day, and you're going to find them at any of these places.

The Money Bar and Beach Club $$

Milkshakes, blended juices with fresh fruit or milk, smoothies, or if you just ask, they will put together any concoction you request. I'm not sure if they are any better or worse than anywhere else, but I have had a couple while cycling the island in brief stops here, and the fruit shakes were great!

Phone: 52-987-869-5140

(Just a couple miles at most south of the last cruise ship)

Cali Café $

The folks here will make you any smoothie you want actually, but on the menu, they have a Green Smoothie with pear, spinach, pecans, milk, and some other stuff, as well as their Peanut Butter Cup or Mango smoothie. All will be refreshing and delicious at this fun little café.

Phone: 52-987-872-6275

(A.R. Salas, between 10 & 15)

Rock 'N Java $$

The milkshakes here, ranging from strawberry to peanut butter are a treat, or they will concoct practically any smoothie which you request. They offer lots of refreshing delights off the menu, but the frozen lemonade with real strawberries is excellent and a bit of a surprise down in Cozumel.

Phone: 52-987-872-4405

(On the main drag just south of Punta Langosta)

Maple Bakehouse $

Their excellence and details never stop, from the food items to the wonderful array of baked goods. If you crave a smoothie, stop in either location and they will prepare nearly any request depending on available ingredients. They understand the art of smoothies!

Phone: 52-987-869-2418

(In town near the water on 6, between Melgar and 5, or on 30, between 17 and 19)

ICE CREAM AND DESSERT TREATS

It seems like the race is on as every restaurant, whether elegant and gourmet or not, has their own proprietary desserts, and most are amazing, to say the least. It's like who can outdo the next with something more delectable than the other. You could go wild tasting the endless extravagant and more simple dessert choices this island continually provides on a seemingly always evolving basis.

Buccanos $$

Becoming one of Cozumel's "must-visits," either for breakfast, lunch, or dinner, or even for a day at the beach, or an evening for two and a very good wine list. A friend of mine on the island has become very fond of Buccanos Granny Smith Apple Parfait with cinnamon ice cream. She is a dessert expert! Buccanos has a large selection of amazing desserts from the simplest of ice creams, to flan, to Granny Smith!

Phone: 044-987-114-5607

(On the main road a couple of miles at the most north of the airport road)

La Chef $$

Having recently moved to their new location on the waterfront, La Chef only continues its excellence and quality. Standard desserts here include their delicious Chocolate Mousse, and La Chef's own Crème Brulee, but the menu here will change at times, with daily specials and surprises.

Phone: 52-987-878-4391

(Rafael Melgar, between 4 & 6)

Azul Madera $$

Complement what will be one of your best meals on the island with one of their marvelous desserts, or stop in late for nothing but dessert and one of their good selection of wines or sangria. Their signature dessert might be the Brioche French Toast doused with cream and coconut ice cream, but more treats await you. A fabulous rich cheesecake with seasonal fruit or berries, lemon, and chocolate ice cream, and a few other flavors, or an assortment of brownies (have ice cream on top), and their Chocolate Mousse.

Phone: 52-987-872-2708

(Calle 3, between 5 & 10)

Guidos $$

If I didn't know any better, I would think this place specialized in desserts, wait, maybe they do? They are amazing, and the ideal end to a graceful and lovely night out in one of the island's best and longest-standing waterfront restaurants. Along with what is one of the island's best wine lists, and their signature sangria, the desserts are sensational and homemade.

Chocolate Mousse yes, an array of ice creams, cheesecakes made in-house, cream pies, a toffee cake, brownies served with select ice creams or custard, and the list goes on. As much care and skill go into the preparation of their desserts as everything else in this Cozumel institution!

Phone: 52-987-872-0946

(Rafael Melgar, between 6 & 8)

New Especias $$

Ice creams, gelatos, a Crème Brulee with pistachios and ginger, or the Italian dessert Tiramisu, a rich and creamy layered coffee infused treat, and maybe their signature, a Grand Marnier Fruit Flambe with vanilla ice cream. Everything here is something very special.

Phone: 52-987-869-7947

(Calle 3, between 5 & 10)

Kondesa $$

This place is elegant in a funky way, beautiful especially after dark, and the presentation of everything is artistic and creative, to say the least. They have a dessert sampler with churros (a Mexican traditional fried dough pastry, which originated in Portugal), coconut ice cream, some sort of sweet corn concoction, and something else, all amazing. If you don't have that much room, settle for any of their suggestions, or the churros, you cannot go wrong!

Phone: 52-987-869-1086

(Ave. 5, between 5 & 7)

The Key Lime Pie Factory $$

My personal favorite! So, you can order this wonderful Key Lime Pie from either of the Lobster House Restaurants next door, yes there are 2 of them, or as explained to me by the owner of the restaurant, he opened this place for his wife because the Key Lime pie was so very, very popular! There are 2 sizes, and it is delicious for the Key Lime Pie lover like me.

Phone: 52-987-120-1399

(A couple of miles north along the main road from the airport road)

Cielito Lindo Restaurant $

The Key Lime Pie here is different than The Key Lime Pie Factory but excellent!

Phone: 52-987-869-2031

(Northwest corner of calle 3 and 5)

Sky Reef $

The banana splits at this cool little beach club and snorkeling mecca are incredible.

(Just a couple miles down the old road, on the west side of the island, from Punta Langosta)

Bella Vita $

A tiny little gelato shop just a block off the square, Bella Vita's products are handmade daily. Somewhat different than ice cream, gelato uses more milk and less cream, and the churning process is slower than that of ice cream, resulting in a somewhat different texture. The results here are wonderful. Mint, chocolate, vanilla, and a handful of other flavors that will change by the season due to availability.

(Calle 2, between 5 & 10)

FINEST WINE SELECTIONS

I am not going to go into any detail here, because I don't drink wine and I know nothing about it. Let me say though, that it was not too long ago when a good bottle of wine was very difficult to find on this island for obvious reasons. The supply chain and availability from Playa Del Carmen to Cancun has changed. While you won't find selections as you might in NYC, or Carmel, California, those in Cozumel's best restaurants have improved dramatically. Chilean, Argentine, and California wines are finding their way, as well as other selections. I will simply list those establishments on the island where you will find the best choices, enjoy your wine!

Sorrisi Restaurant $$
Phone: 52-987-869-0960
(Calle 3, between R. Melgar and 5)

Buccanos $$
Phone: 044-987-114-5607
(A short drive, maybe a 1/2 mile north of the airport road on the main road)

Guidos Restaurant $$
Phone: 52-987-872-0946
(Rafael Melgar, between 6 & 8)

La Cocay $
Phone: 52-987-872-5533
(Calle 8 between 10 & 15)

New Especias $$
Phone: 52-987-869-7947
(Calle 3, between 5 & 10)

Cielito Lindo $
Phone: 52-987-869-2031
(Northwest corner of calle 3 and 5)

Pepe's $$
Phone: 52-987-872-0213
(Near the corner of Rafael Melgar and A. R. Salas)

Panchos Backyard $$
(On Rafael Melgar, between 8 & 10)

The Money Bar and Beach Club $$
Phone: 52-987-869-5140
(A short drive south of the last cruise ship pier, by a mile or two along the old road)

Azul Madera $$
Phone: 52-987-872-2708
(Calle 3, between 5 & 10)

La Chef $$
Phone: 52-987-878-4391
(Rafael Melgar, between 4 & 6)

Casa Mission $$
Phone: 52-987-872-1641
(Corner of Benito Juarez and Ave. 55)

El Palomar $$
Phone: 52-987-120-2792
(Corner of Rafael Melgar and 10)

BEST BLOODY MARYS

There are a few here that stand tall above the rest. All are different as is always the case with Bloodys. They are still not an institution here as they may be in Milwaukee or East Lansing, Michigan!

Mezcalitos $$

Phone: 52-987-876-0914

(On the east side right where the transversal road meets the east side)

Coconuts Bar and Restaurant $$

Phone: 52-987-100-5266

(Also on the east side about a mile south of the transversal road)

Rock 'N Java $$

Phone: 52-987-872-4405

(Rafael Melgar, just south of Punta Langosta)

The Money Bar and Beach Club $$

Phone: 52-987-869-5140

(A mile or a bit more south of the last cruise ship pier along the old road)

Jeanie's Waffle House $$

Phone: 52-987- 878-4647

(Rafael Melgar, just south of Punta Langosta)

Flamingo Hotel $$

Phone: 52-987-872-1264

(Calle 6 norte, between Rafael Melgar and 5)

La Chef $$

Phone: 52-987-878-4391

(Rafael Melgar, between 4 & 6)

Buccanos $$

Phone: 044-987-114-5607

(On the main ocean road, about a mile north of the airport road)

El Palomar $$

Phone: 52-987-120-2792

(Rafael Melgar and 10)

BEST MARGARITAS AND MOJITOS

I could make note of probably 50 places in Cozumel with remarkable takes on this classic Mexican cocktail, but I won't. There are just too many that are just too good. So, if it is a margarita or mojito you are after, definitely give these a try, but listen to fellow travelers and their advice, your margarita/mojito senses will guide you to even more. There are no mixes in this crowd!

Casa Mission $$

An old Cozumel elegant destination that has wonderful traditional margaritas, and very strong Cadillac Margaritas. They know how to entertain their guests!

Phone: 52-987-872-1641
(Corner of Benito Juarez and Ave 55)

Wet Wendy's $$

To many, this is the home of the Cozumel margarita and they are delicious! Stick to the essential, the traditional Mexican margarita, with or without salt, or be adventurous and explore one of their many different takes on this classic drink. Everything is fresh, with real ingredients, which is the case with all of these in this list. You won't find a mix anywhere!

Basil margaritas, coconut, pear, mango, pineapple, cilantro, honey and several more, and they all have their followers

(Just north by ½ a block on the pedestrian walk from the square)

La Casa Del Mojito $

The baby sister of Wet Wendy's, and while the margaritas are really good here, it is the mojitos this place specializes in, as well as great Cuban food, AND real Cuban cigars. Classic Cuban mojitos along with several twists like the Monkey Mojito with banana, a Mango Mojito, and for all football fans, the Green Bay Mojito infused with melon, or the Caribbean with coconut, an Italian with Frangelico, and even an Almond Mojito with Amaretto. You get the picture, so stop in and enjoy some of the best.

(On 5, between Rosado Salas and 3)

The Liquor Box $

This very rustic beach bar on the east side of the island may just trump them all when it comes to Mojitos and Margaritas, they are phenomenal, strong, inexpensive, and large! Reminiscent of the east side beach bars on this side years ago, as many (there are only about 8) have expanded since the last hurricane to a point never before seen on this side of the island, ever. Still, there is no electricity on this side of Cozumel, everything is run by a generator, and cell service is non-existent. Regardless, also known as "Welcome to Miami," this spot is a sleeper and the drinks are very special, enjoy. Everything on this side of Cozumel closes typically by 5:00 p.m.

(Just north of the southern end on the east side)

El Palomar $$

Artisanal cocktails and delectable food are the norms in this classic old Cozumel building housing the fabulous El Palomar Restaurant. The mojitos are wonderful as are the margaritas, from a traditional lime-based to their Strawberry or Mango Margarita. Sit on the old front porch or in the side bar and they will create something delightful for you.

Phone: 52-987-120-2792
(Rafael Melgar on the corner of 10)

Casa Denis $

The oldest restaurant on the island has had plenty of time to hone their skills, and they create from scratch, one of the finest margaritas in Cozumel. Sit outside along the pedestrian walk and watch the island stroll by.

Phone: 52-987-872-0067
(On the pedestrian walk leaving the southeast corner of the town square)

La Choza $

Another of the islands old time restaurants and they continue to wow customers with generations-old Mexican recipes, and some of the island's best margaritas. A delicious meal here is not complete without a classic La Choza margarita.

Phone: 52-987-872-0958
(On 10, between A. R. Salas and 3 sur)

El Moro $

Yet another of Cozumel's oldest establishments, they too serve up a traditional margarita that is pure Mexico.

Phone: 52-987-872-3029
(On 75 biz, between 2 & 4)

The (2) Lobster Houses $

Both Fernando's Lobster House and the original directly next door, are famous for not only their lobster recipes and the Key Lime Pie, but for their margaritas. I like to go out in the evening sometimes and just sit at either bar and enjoy the quiet of this end of the island with a refreshing and strong margarita.

Phone: 52-987-107-3116
(On the north end maybe 2 miles north of the airport road on the main drag)

Sky Reef Beach Bar $$

If you come out for a nice shore access snorkel, or by boat here, when finished be sure to try one of their yummy margaritas.

(About 2 miles south of the last cruise ship pier on the old road)

Mezcalito's $$

One would be completely remiss if this age-old east side bar was excluded from this list. Their selection and preparation of a classic margarita is astounding. Stay off scooters if you plan to have more than one, these margaritas pack a bunch.

Phone: 52-987-876-0914
(Right at the end of the transversal road as you meet the east side of the island)

Señor Iguanas $$

Directly south of Mezcalito's is another of the east sides long time little beach bars with equally magnificent, and traditionally prepared margaritas. Not too much of this and not too much of that, they are consistently excellent.

Phone: 52-987-105-6344
(Just south of Mezcalito's)

Woody's $$

Conveniently located a block east of the Playa Del Carmen ferry pier is Woody's, with the longest daily hours of operation probably on the island. Your margarita will be waiting for you daily from 9:30-12:00, and they are open Saturdays I think until 2:00 a.m. Traditional, or selections including mango, strawberry, banana, tamarindo with chile, and peach, and I am probably missing a couple. Live music daily AND all day.

(Just off the northeast corner of the square, next to 7 Eleven)

Kinta $$

Simply wonderful margaritas, as is everything else at this quirky and beautiful spot, especially after the sun goes down. Great for a nice evening meal, or a seat and appetizer with another of the island's best margaritas.

Phone: 52-987-869-0544

(On 5, between 2 & 4)

La Perlita $

Quiet and a bit out of the way, yet the astonishing and authentic seafood dishes beckon all those who wish for a Cozumel meal in a Cozumel old-time setting. Family recipes have held court here for a long time, including their margaritas. Everything here is well worth the bit of a trek. An inexpensive cab ride or an energetic stroll. Closes around 8:00 p.m.

Phone: 52-987-869-8343

(Ave. 65 & 10)

La Chef $$

Sit out front here for a sunset at their new location along the waterfront and select an appetizer and one of the island's best margaritas. If it isn't a sunset you want, no harm as La Chef is open breakfast, lunch, and dinner with fantastic hand-crafted meals.

Phone: 52-987-878-4391

(Rafael Melgar, between 4 & 6)

"The time is always right to do what is right"

Martin Luther King

INCREDIBLE VIEWS OR DINING NEAR THE WATER

Hemmingway's $$

One of the several large palapa covered restaurant/bars north of the ferry pier to Playa Del Carmen, Hemmingway's is available for breakfast, lunch, and dinner, and a lot more happens here! A beautiful spot for an unobstructed sunset, the view day or night is breathtaking as you are directly on the water. Live music or a DJ's going well into the night, with fun dancing. The pulse here can get pretty lively later in the evenings.

Phone: 52-987-688-1634

(1/4 mile north of the ferry pier and town square)

La Monina $$

Another one of the gorgeous palapa bars north of the ferry pier, La Monina is close by Hemmingway's. Excellent food day and night, a galaxy of available cocktails, and a bit more intimate of a setting. The views and sunsets from this funky establishment are special. Watch the fishing and dive boats come in for the night, and gaze at the sun dropping over the mainland horizon as night falls.

Phone: 52-987-872-5762

(1/4 mile north of the ferry pier and town square)

Shakas $$

Yet another of these lovely palapa restaurants set directly on Cozumel's waterfront, looking across the water toward Playa Del Carmen (11 miles away), and seemingly a world apart from the hectic streets of Playa. Shakas is a beach club and restaurant/bar, that is also a sunset lover's dream.

(1/4 mile north of the ferry pier and town square)

Shii Fu $$

As you dine in this peaceful atmosphere, with impeccably prepared and presented Asian influenced food, and the elegant surroundings, your view matches the serenity of this establishment. Reserve a spot if it's a sunset you want to see, or if it is the dancing lights of boats across the water at night, a reservation may also be a good idea as Shii Fu is a popular and simply stunning location.

Phone: 52-987-114-5607

(About 1.5 miles north of the Playa Del Carmen ferry pier on the only road north)

Buccanos $$

The sister restaurant to Shii Fu, in the same complex, Buccanos is equally as lovely with stunning views, and a perfect spot for a sunset meal and cocktail, or a bite to eat later in the evening. Buccanos is an enticing stop during the day as well, whether you spend the day at the beach club, or stop in for a hearty breakfast, or an elegantly prepared lunch. One of the island's most well-appointed restaurants with exquisitely prepared meals and the views are to die for.

Phone: 044-987-114-5607

(About 1.5 miles north of the Playa Del Carmen ferry pier on the only road north)

Playa Corona $

A somewhat quiet beach bar compared to some of the larger on the island, with excellent shore access snorkeling just a short swim out to a well-protected reef. The owner is very conscientious and concerned about your safety and the protection of the shallow reef close by. There is a small sand beach, a palapa covered area for a wonderful lunch, or a swim and a relaxed serene day on the shores of Cozumel. One of the islands loveliest spots for lunch or an afternoon cocktail in a peaceful island setting far from any big crowds.

(Just south of Chankanaab Park, a mile or so south of Puerta Maya cruise ship pier)

No Name Bar $$

In town and very popular, but if it's an exciting pulse you are after with a pool, no beach, but directly on the water, No Name is very cool and ideal for a sunset. As recently as 15 years ago, the snorkeling and coral off here were magnificent. Most of that is gone, but some decent snorkeling and fish remain. No Name is very popular with cruise ship crews and some of the younger crowd. The cocktails are excellent, the place hops, and IF there is no cruise ship in the way, the sunsets can be amazing.

Phone: 52-987-878-4020

(Just south of Punta Langosta cruise ship pier)

The Money Bar $$

Just south of the Puerta Maya cruise ship pier, after the old road splits to the right is this ever-popular beach bar that is as popular by day as it is by night. No cruise ships will ever be docked in your way, if you come to view a sunset. Live music many nights, sunset BBQ's, and during the day this place is by no means a quiet beach bar, it has crowds though not bad, the views day and night are quite special. Decent shore access snorkeling and good food with kickin cocktails!

Phone: 52-987-869-5140

(Maybe a mile south of the Puerta Maya cruise ship pier on the old road)

El Pescador $$

For excellent food, gorgeous coves, quiet beaches, and sort of a mix of crowds, the serenity of the lovely east side of the island, El Pescador may be the ultimate combination. It is remote and remarkably beautiful, and here you get the best of both worlds with attentive service, and feet in the sand dining with the Caribbean just steps away. It is also the surfing home and island surf school of the islands surf pioneer, Nacho and Cozumel Surfing.

Phone: 52-987-872-7440

(About ½ way down the east coast road, impossible to miss)

Coconuts $$

The hilltop and jungle retreat of Coconuts is unique on the island. It is the highest point in elevation on Cozumel. Sitting atop a cliff overlooking the blue spectacular waters of the Caribbean, there is nothing like a lunch or late afternoon dinner at Coconuts. Things close here on the east side in the late afternoon, so your time here is done usually by 5:30 p.m. at the latest, but you will be treated to some of the island's most magnificent Caribbean views.

Phone: 52-987-100-5266

(Nearly ½ way down the east coast road, also impossible to miss)

COZUMEL'S NIGHTLIFE/DANCING/LIVE MUSIC

Woody's $$

Literally all day here along the pedestrian walk you will find live music. Beginning in the morning, solo artists will perform throughout the day, culminating with bands well into the night. There are lots of tables outdoors, the food is good and the cocktails flow. Just off the town square and a block from the main drag and the Playa Del Carmen ferry pier, come gather here at one of the island's most popular hangouts.

(Just off the northeast corner of the square)

Wet Wendy's $$

Wet Wendy's mixes up an array of excellent margaritas, a large food menu, and plenty of room for after-dark dancing to salsa, rock 'n roll and jazz nearly nightly, particularly during the high season. Also, just off the pedestrian walk, the open-air vibe here has been entertaining island guests for years. Plenty of room for dancing. The big sister of La Casa Del Mojito, on the other side of the square, with mojitos, Cuban cigars, and excellent Cuban sandwiches.

(A ½ block north of the square on the pedestrian walk)

Blue Angel Resort and Dive Shop $$

Few spots on Cozumel rival the intimacy and view as do evenings here when they have live music. Typically, only on weekends, and it is seasonally dependent, but during the high season this is a beautiful spot for a cocktail and a night of music.

Phone: 52-987-872-0819

(About 1.5 miles south of the Playa Del Carmen ferry pier on the main road)

Viva Mexico $$

Head upstairs to this little restaurant with stunning views across the street from the water. On weekends, favorite local bands perform here, and this place rocks until late into the night. Sit back and enjoy or dance the night away. Drinks are a bit pricey, but for a night out the atmosphere is really nice especially if you're a music fan.

(Corner of Rafael Melgar and Salas)

Hemmingway's $$

Hemmingway's is simply stunning after dark under the large open-air palapa. North of town by a bit, the setting is quiet, directly looking over the water and festive with flickering lights, a large dance floor, and great music most weekends.

Phone: 52-987-688-1634

(A ½ mile north of the square right on the water)

Hotel Flamingo $

Soft jazz and a cozy setting with excellent margaritas are what you will find at this small boutique hotel downtown. The Flamingo has always been a favorite stop of mine. A ½ block off the main drag, yet seemingly far from it as you step into this modest and engaging island stop. Live music in an intimate venue most weekends.

Phone: 52-987-872-1264

(Calle 6 just east of the main drag and the waterfront)

Beds and Friends Hostel $

More for the younger crowd of international travelers, but Sundays after 3:00 p.m. you will usually find live music at this impeccable and welcoming island youth hostel. Located in a quiet neighborhood a short walk from the square, Beds and Friends is one of the best youth hostels I have ever encountered. All are welcome.

(On the southwest corner of 10 and 10)

The Money Bar $$

A popular spot well away from town along the old island road south of town. Consistently a fun spot for dancing and live music on weekends. Open-air and along the waterfront, have a cab bring you out for a night of dancing under the stars.

Phone: 52-987-869-5140

(A mile maybe south of Puerta Maya cruise ship port, the first place you will see on the old road)

SPENDING IDLE TIME

THE MAIN TOWN OF SAN MIGUEL

There are only 2 towns on Cozumel, though San Miguel is the only town on the island of any significance. The other is the tiny enclave of El Cedral which will be discussed later, but El Cedral is the home to some cool little houses, meandering residential streets, a small chapel, some shopping, tequila tasting, and Kun Che Park.

San Miguel on the other hand is a thriving and growing metropolis of around 100,000 people. The center of San Miguel is the ferry pier from Playa Del Carmen, and Benito Juarez Park, or the town square. It is from here that the town goes west a couple of miles, north toward the quiet northern Hotel Zone and Cozumel Country Club (the islands lone golf course) 4 miles or so, and south through the busy 3 cruise ship ports, a distance of 5 miles or so.

San Miguel is home to a remarkable array of restaurants featuring everything from elegant dining to local taquerias and street food stands, all are delicious depending on your mood. You will find Italian, fresh seafood, artisanal cuisine, sushi, Lebanese, authentic and traditional Yucatecan cuisine, and nearly anything in between. You will find quiet neighborhoods for a long walk and the busiest of streets buzzing with activity. Shop till your heart's content at the many little spots around the square, and up and down the main drag of Rafael Melgar. The majority of your shopping will be found in a relatively short stretch from the renowned Los Cinco Soles on the corner of Rafael Melgar and calle 8, south to Punta Langosta cruise ship pier along the waterfront and throughout the pedestrian walks around the square.

San Miguel is the home to dozens of world-class dive shops, 2 cinemas, a planetarium, several churches, and a museum just north of the ferry pier which just reopened in February of 2020 after a 2-year remodel. While exploring the town, the further east you walk, the more local it becomes. This is a good thing, as the streets are safe, and you will find bakeries, small shops, and scores of local restaurants day and night, hosted by families who have been graciously serving visitors in many cases for decades. The sense of community on the island is alive and well, it is one of this destination's strongest attributes. The local islanders welcome you as they go about their lives, with the ever-present tourism and the challenges it brings to the island. This is their home, but you are so very welcome!

The Malecon (a waterfront walkway), runs north and a bit south of the Playa ferry pier and is an ideal morning or evening walk, or the perfect spot for a Cozumel sunset. This is San Miguel, and you will learn far more as you explore the pages of this book.

OUT-OF-THE-WAY BEACH BARS

In this section, we will discuss smaller beach bars, all without an entry fee, except for Punta Sur Park. There may be charges at some for a lounge chair and some other ancillary items, like fishing or snorkel excursions, but for the most part, aside from food and drink, these are all free to explore and enjoy with crowds far less than those which will be discussed in the next section.

Playa Chen Rio $$

On the incredibly scenic and more remote east side of the island, Chen Rio is one of the most popular and stunning stretches of beach on the island. It will be crowded on Sundays as this is kind of a local's day off, but still, there is plenty of room. Any other day and it may seem like you are alone out here! Explore the numerous tidal pools where the snorkeling is quite good, walk the beaches, play in the shallow water coves, have some of the best seafood on the island at Restaurant El Pescador, or bring a cooler and a towel and plop down at this beautiful spot. The beach is free, but rental lounges are available for a nominal fee. Cash only, there is no electricity, everything is run by generator and the restaurant opens around 10:30 a.m. and closes by 5ish. The home of Cozumel's surfing pioneer, and Nachos Cozumel Surfing School.

www.cozumelsurfing.com

(2/3 of the way down the east coast road from the south end, impossible to miss)

Playa San Martin

A long and windswept stretch of beach that goes on for miles. Like any of the east side beaches, always be aware of rip tides and undercurrents. Playa San Martin is good about displaying their water safety flag, and if the flag is red, be extremely careful swimming. With that said, this a gorgeous spot. Park along the road and bring a cooler, beach towels and enjoy a day at one of the island's best beaches. Unless the water is extremely calm and they display the green flag (safe conditions), snorkeling is out of the question, if the green flag is up, the snorkeling will surprise you here. There is a restaurant across the street with amazing views. No charge.

(1/2 way down the east side road from either end, you will see the signs)

Punta Morena Beach Bar

In the not too distant past, all of these little beach bars on the east side were simple and rustic, with no electricity (there still isn't), but since the last hurricane years ago, the infrastructure on a couple of them, including Punta Morena has really grown. A long beach, with some shallow coves, volleyball nets, hammocks strung throughout, excellent food at the little restaurant, and even a couple of little dipping pools for hot feet, or the young kids.

Phone: 52-987-876-1225

(3/4 of the way down the east side from the southern end, impossible to miss)

Punta Sur Park $$

Much more than just a beach, Punta Sur Park is one of the island's most sensational and most scenic destinations! There is an entrance fee of around $14.00, but it is beyond worth it for the day. The park encompasses the entire southern point of the island where you will find a lighthouse, 3 lagoons, amazing bird-life, particularly November – March, with flamingoes, roseate spoonbills, great white egrets, and many other species, thick jungle, some ruins, a healthy crocodile population if you look carefully, boardwalks and a watchtower, a small maritime museum and a couple of beach bars at the end of the road (the road is about 4–5 miles to where it dead-ends). The beach at the end of the road is breathtaking and the swimming is nearly always calm and very safe, with incredibly good snorkeling out maybe a 2-minute swim. The beaches on your left as you enter the park are off-limits to people as they are part of the park's concerted efforts at protecting the nesting sites of several species of sea turtles who come back annually to the same spot to nest and lay their eggs. Much of the island's east side is off-limits during nesting season to protect the nests.

Phone: 52-987-872-1522

(The southern point of the island)

Playa Palancar $$$

Of the many beach bars on the west side of the island, Playa Palancar is the last before you reach the end of the island and is the furthest from town, but it is well worth the visit. You are no longer allowed cars or scooters at the entrance along the old road, from here the old road is blocked and only for bicycle use. When continuing south from here you will be forced to merge onto the new road. There is no entrance fee and do not bring your own food as it is not allowed. You could spend the day here conceivably and not spend a dime, but chances are you will want to eat or have a cold drink, all you need is here. The hours daily are 9:00 a.m.–5:00 p.m. and the beach is beautiful and typically calm. Swim out to what is so-so snorkeling, or around $20.00 will get you a small boat, equipment, and a short ride to far better snorkeling. $10.00 will get you a chair and umbrella on the beach, the grounds here are very nice, and kayaks or paddleboards are available for rent.

Quiet compared to the larger clubs on this side of the island, not as many toys, far more relaxing and simply beautiful.

(About a 25-minute cab, scooter or drive in a rental car)

Playa Azul $

Playa Azul is a tiny little beach bar up in the northern hotel zone of Cozumel, but the accommodations make up for its small size. There is no admission, the beach is quite small and cozy, but there is a pool, a palapa covered dining area with decent enough food, a small but nice stretch of beach with crystal clear water for swimming and good snorkeling out front. They do sometimes require a small minimum of a couple of hundred pesos for the use of beach chairs and such, but this can change depending on the season and crowd. The restrooms are very clean, with outdoor showers to rinse off the salt, and there is a resident dive shop to book scuba trips, snorkel excursions, and even some fishing. Playa Azul is very nice, simple, and rarely too crowded.

Phone: 52-987-869-5175

(About 3.5 miles north of town close to the golf course)

Playa Corona $$

These next two little beach bars are among my favorite on the island for lots of reasons, and the snorkeling offshore is certainly one of those reasons. Playa Corona has tables in the sand and a stone wall at the water, with some wide steps for water access, so while there is sand it isn't a beach per se, but do not let this keep you away! The water is gorgeous, and the shore access snorkeling is as colorful and fish-filled as nearly any on the island. Lots of umbrellas, small palapas, a few hammocks here and there are plenty of lounge chairs to ease away the day. Delicious ceviche's and fresh seafood are another plus to spending the day at this lovely little out of the way Cozumel beach bar.

(About 2 miles south of Punta Langosta cruise ship pier)

Sky Reef $$

Sky Reef is sort of like Playa Corona, just a bit larger. A delightfully friendly staff, excellent food, shore access snorkeling as good as anywhere, plenty of shade and sand at your feet. Smaller again than some of the island's larger beach clubs, but it is a quiet and stunning option for a day of snorkeling, swimming, maybe a soothing massage in one of their several open-air massage cabanas, or just a great lunch and a cold cocktail. Fairly close to town, but the feel is far away. Showers, dressing rooms and lockers, lots of room to spread out, snorkel gear to rent, or bring your own.

Stop and admire one of the loveliest little seaside chapels you will see anywhere, just next door!

www.skyreefcozumel.com
(Just south of Playa Corona by a few minutes)

ALL-INCLUSIVE BEACH BARS

This section will cover the beach clubs that you will find south of the last cruise ship pier (Puerta Maya), along the old island west coast road. You will be directed toward this road just south of Punta Langosta by well-displayed signage, as to where the road splits off from the new road. Follow the sign to Chankanaab Park and you will be on your way to any of these. The road ends some 15 miles south of where you enter and will merge back onto the new road right at Palancar Beach Club.

The following are in order from north to south as you follow the road south. Beginning with San Francisco Beach further north, to Alberto's near the south end. These in this section are for the most part far more commercialized, typically include an entry fee and will be pricier than the last section, though with more infrastructure, pools,

inflatable water toys, parasailing, shopping, sea kayaks, glass-bottom boats, and even very high-end beach cabana options for couples that include private pools, couples massage, king-size beds and accommodations for the day, well deserving of a romantic escape or honeymoon luxury. Some are far more crowded than others, some have better beaches, and some will price you to death. We will do our best to steer you in the right direction if this is the type of experience you desire. Pricing can be all over the place, or inconsistent due to the high or low season. I will hesitate for the most part to include pricing though some will be included. I highly encourage you if visiting any of these next places to visit their websites and determine your price categories.

San Francisco Beach Club

I believe this is the oldest of these All-Inclusives on the island, it dates to 1970. There is an entrance fee of around $20.00 and it goes from there depending on your choice of food and drinks, choice of lounge chairs, umbrellas, and so on. The beach is ok, but not large and with all the lounge chairs, it gets even smaller. There is a small pool and a ton of other activities to spend your money on from, glass-bottom boat rides, jet skis, plastic sea kayak rentals, inflatable water toys and slides, and snorkel tours. The food is marginal and the drinks about the same. Relaxation seems difficult to come by here as it is always crowded.

Phone: 52-987-118-6236

Carlos N Charlies Beach Club

Just south of San Francisco is Carlos n Charlies. The entrance here is free, but all else is going to cost you, from a lounge chair to an umbrella, etc. The beach here is a bit better and they are open at night as well, with live music, dancing, and dinner during a sunset. All-day passes are available for food and drinks, beach lounges, and water toys. The beach volleyball scene here is crazy fun, and jet skis, parasailing, and sea kayaks are available for rent.

Phone: 52-987-564-0960

Paradise Beach

Paradise Beach is just south of the above, and in my opinion, the best of these three. There are small paths to stroll through the property with some cute little shops, the grounds here are quite lovely. The heart-shaped pool is awesome with seats all around and a swim-up bar. The entrance fee is something like $3.00 which gets you pool and beach access. Another $10.00 or so gets you a beach chair and umbrella. The beach here is very nice, and the All-Inclusive price of around $55.00 per person gives you access to everything, including playing on the inflatable water slides and trampolines, plus unlimited food and drink. The AI price drops for younger children. There are separate passes for just water toys and sea kayaks and such. Paradise is a bit more spread out, nice for couples and even families who might want a little more room to maneuver. The pool here is wonderful.

Phone: 52-987-689-0010

Playa Mia

The sky is the limit here, not only for your pocketbook but also for entertainment for the family, sort of like a tropical Wisconsin Dells or Coney Island! After an entry fee of $35.00ish, the parasailing is $65.00, a ½ hour on a wave runner will set you back $65.00. Granted, the entry fee gains you access to a maze of small kid-friendly pools with water slides, and an equally large collection of water toys, slides, walkways and trampolines off the beach, kayaks, and paddleboards, yet it can be a cluster %@*?!& here! It seems like everyone wants a tip, the beach isn't huge by any imagination and the vendors are a bit too harassing for my taste. With that said, if you have a family, and younger kids that need this down in Mexico, you will find a totally fun day in the sun here!

Mr. Sanchos

Sort of a grownups Playa Mia with a gorgeous property, lush foliage, massage tables, a nice pool with a swim-up bar, hammocks, a decent beach, all the inflated water toys, and for $60.00 AI for endless food and drink, and access to all the above, it isn't a bad deal. Price drops per the age of your kids. Very commercialized which doesn't do much for me, but then again it isn't about me! Their Spa Suites are something that for now sets this place apart for couples looking for something very romantic. As of now,

I do not believe they are available for overnight stays, but that would be the ultimate especially for the $500.00 price tag! The price though does get you all you can eat and drink, a one-hour couples massage, your own private beach cabana, small private pool, a king-size bed, AC, a 60" TV (not sure why you would want that), and many other amenities.

Phone: 52-987-120-2220

Nachi Cocom

Relatively new (maybe 14 years), Nachi Cocom is a bit different from the rest of these AI beach bars, and the property is quite beautiful. First, they limit the daily entrance to 140 people. Open from 9:00 a.m.–5:00 p.m. daily, reservations are encouraged, and $60.00 will gain you access to a wonderful beach, a beautiful pool with a swim-up bar, hot tub, and unlimited excellent food and drink. For this type of beach club, with these amenities, offering a guaranteed relatively quiet day, Nachi Cocom is somewhat unique. Kids under 3 are free, and the price goes up according to age and tops out at $60.00. Massages are available as are snorkel tours at an additional price. I remember when this place first opened and you could just walk in, enjoy the beach and pool with the purchase of food and drink, it was amazing then as it is now. For an all-inclusive beach resort, this is Cozumel's most secluded and quietest.

Alberto's Beach Bar & Grill

"The best tail I ever had," is their motto, and yes, the food is excellent here, including the fresher than fresh lobster tails! No cover to enter the property, but all-inclusive options are available for food/drink and other beach club activities. They do stay open evenings with amazing candlelit sunset dinners on the beach, and once again, the food here is surprisingly delicious, but it is not remotely cheap. Alberto's has 3 locations on the island, but this is their one beach access. During the day, they have a nice beach, snorkel excursions, parasailing, glass-bottom boat rides, wave runners of course, and beach massages. One delightful thing here is no solicitors hitting you up with little bracelets and trinkets. Great beach volleyball with a young crowd daily. A highlight here for sure is the outstanding food and the opportunity to view a sunset in a somewhat remote island location, with the beach dinner, and hopefully, it isn't windy! The Key Lime Pie is a secret here worth discovering!

Phone: 52-987-876-1394

SPAS AND GREAT MASSAGES

There are many spots to enjoy a soothing massage on the island. Most beach clubs offer a calming and quiet location in the shade for a massage, and there are a handful of island spas, though, one in particular has received accolades throughout the Caribbean and on Cozumel, and that is Barefoot in Cozumel. I have only had experience with Barefoot and I will discuss below. I will mention a few others I have heard great things about, as well as some that are in simply beautiful locations.

Barefoot in Cozumel

Owned and operated by long time island resident Sally Hurwitch, or Amethyst Amatista on Facebook, she has received many awards for her Reiki therapy and Ashiatsu Barefoot Massage. By appointment only, go to her website and read about her work, then set up a date and receive an hour of the most relaxing tissue massage, or energy healing. I have known Sally's world for many years has been all about her practice, her spirituality, and giving back to the community of Cozumel.

https://www.barefootincozumel.com/

Temazcal Cenote Experience

I will preface by saying I have never been here, or do I know how to get there, but I have heard nothing but rave reviews about the time spent here! Located in the Cozumel jungle on a private ranch, you will experience the ancient spiritual healing of Mayan Temazcal. A steam lodge and a dip in the chilly cenote, as well as hiking through the property are only a portion of the unrivaled adventure one will discover with the Temazcal Experience. This is a step back into the ancient world of the Maya, on a part of the island only the adventurous will see or seek out.

F@Mayan.Steam.Lodge.Cozumel

Bliss Day Spa

This is a full-service spa offering deep tissue massage, Mayan massage, facials, Hot Stone Therapy, and much, much more. Located in a comfortable setting right in town, the therapy and massage work of the professionals at Bliss Day Spa are said to be outstanding. The place is small, but the service is excellent.

http://www.blissdayspacozumel.com/eng/
(On 1, between 5 & 10)

***These are a few beach clubs where the location is just beautiful for a quiet massage outside in the tropical breeze.**

- **Buccanos Beach Club (www.buccanos.com)**
- **Punta Morena (gorgeous setting on the islands remote east side)**
- **Sky Reef Beach Club (www.skyreefcozumel.com)**
- **Playa Corona Beach Club (quiet and beautiful, just before Sky Reef about 6 miles south of town)**

GREAT PEOPLE WATCHING

I've juggled back and forth as to whether or not to even include this category, but many travelers visit for a short time, and just want to plop down for lunch and a few cocktails and watch the world go by, this is for you. The clear answer is Parque Benito Juarez (the town square), right where the ferry landing is from Playa Del Carmen.

Palmeras Restaurant is right at the ferry pier. The food and drinks are great, it has been there forever, and is a fun spot to sit and watch the curious world of Cozumel clash with visitors trying to figure out where they are going, and the real world of the island graciously dealing with it all. Or wander into the square and take a seat at one of the benches, where you will see tourists beginning their journey, and residents going about their business as they do each day. Shop at the many kiosks dotting the perimeter, or find your way to Woody's, at the northeast corner of the square, and grab a table along the pedestrian walk for a margarita, food across the culinary spectrum, and nearly constant live music from 9:00 a.m.-midnight daily.

GREAT SPOTS FOR A WALK OR A RUN

I'll offer a few suggestions for both the vigorous and not so vigorous, but either way, these are places on the island that offer a little peace and quiet, and a beautiful reflection of what this island is all about. Either of these routes is good for a walk or a run.

From the Playa Del Carmen Ferry Pier North

Begin at the pier and walk as far north as you desire along the water until you reach the Cozumel Country Club, where the road kind of stops. The distance is about 5 miles. This walk round trip is 10 miles or so, but the beauty of it is that you can turn around wherever you like and return. I like the walk from the ferry to Marina Blanco, which is maybe 2 miles one way. Then at the Marina entrance, walk into the parking lot, there is a small store by the boat launch. Buy a beer, or cold drink, and sit in the little area right next to it and watch the boats come and go, spend all the time you want, then head back. If you continue, you will pass private homes, a few looks at the water, hotels, a few beach clubs, and eventually the road ends. If you're pooped, hail a cab and you are back to where you started in the blink of an eye.

The Neighborhoods Off the Water, and North of the Square

There is a particularly quiet area of town a couple of blocks north of the square, north to the airport road, and then from the waterfront east to Ave. 20 or so. This is a part of town with residential homes, B&B's, a few small restaurants, condos, and plain peace and quiet. Either walk north from the square or anywhere east from the waterfront and you will find maybe 15 square blocks of island simplicity and a peaceful walk.

Wander South of the Ferry Pier Along the Water

You could walk a long way from the ferry pier south, literally to the end of the island. But, enjoy this stretch for what it is and maybe take in a mile, or more, with gorgeous views of the waterfront, restaurants, shops, dive centers, pass at least one of the cruise ship piers depending on how long you walk and step into endless places for a rest and a cold drink. The traffic alongside can be a bit hectic on this stretch, though this is still a nice walk or run particularly early mornings.

Anywhere on the Old Road Going South Along the Island's West Coast

The second prettiest stretch of road on the island offers excellent opportunities for a walk or run, about 20 some odd miles of them. Anywhere between Punta Sur and Chankanaab provides you with a quiet stretch of pavement, lots of shade, and yes moments in full sun, but it is lovely in most spots. There are a handful of resorts, small and large beach clubs, private homes, but mostly just a quiet and gorgeous seaside walk or run on a portion of the old island road.

The East Coast Road

Few places in the Caribbean match the stunning views of Cozumel's east coast. If you're on foot though, be prepared, as there is little shade except for the occasional small beach bar, and one little hotel. From Mezcalito's to Punta Sur is about 12 miles, and nearly all of it has 2 parallel roads, the old and the new. The old road is closest to the ocean and is strictly reserved for cyclists and pedestrians. If it isn't a road you want to walk on, this side of the island offers the walker or jogger the longest stretches of uninterrupted beach on Cozumel. There are several long stretches, but San Martin Beach, about halfway down this side of the island goes on for miles.

As a side note, I wanted to mention the following small island park. **Parque "Sacahua" is a tiny triangular park on the airport road at the corner with 15. It is an ideal spot to walk from town and sit to just enjoy the island's peace and quiet. From the town square, it is maybe a 20-minute walk north through a quiet corner of San Miguel.

SPECIAL SITES FOR A SUNRISE

This is a pretty simple category as the only sunrise you will see on the island, is on the east side. Since nothing is open at this time of the morning over there, if you head out for a sunrise, you will be on your own, albeit with any number of others with the same idea. All you will find are 6–7 closed small beach bars (hours for all of them are around 10:00 a.m.–6:00 p.m. daily) and miles of stunning coastline for a remarkable sunrise. There is ONE other possibility on this side of the island, and I encourage anyone to spend the night there, Hotel Ventanas Al Mar. The only hotel on the islands east side, this small boutique hotel is something very special. With 16 some odd rooms, book a night or several here, and you will have the night completely

alone, under a blanket of stars, totally quiet and you will be assured of an amazing Cozumel sunrise.

Beautiful Locations for a Sunset

Literally anywhere on the west side of the island will offer you a tropical sunset over the faraway jungles of the Yucatan mainland. The following are only suggestions, and nothing will be blocking your view, but the options are endless. If for some reason a cruise ship is docked during a sunset, well move on.

- **North of the airport road,** there are several roadside stops where locals gather each evening along the rocky coastline for a sunset. Follow the only road north, pass the marina and you will see a couple of areas along the road with benches and access to the water. Sunsets from here are quiet and beautiful.
- **Along the Malecon,** from the Playa Del Carmen ferry pier north about ¾'s of a mile to Shaka's Palapa Bar, is a long wall along the coast, lots of seating and other options to admire the sun going down, and watching the fishing and dive boats coming in for the night.

- **Follow the old road south,** pass Chankanaab Park, and you will find miles of empty and romantic spots for a sunset. Either enjoy it on your own, or stop at one of several small beach bars, and sit down with a cold cocktail and a view for the ages.
- **Playa Azul Beach Bar,** near the end of the north road, is one of my favorite spots for a cold cocktail and a Cozumel sunset. About 5 miles north of town.
- **La Internacional Cerveceria,** just south of the first cruise ship pier, this home to scores of Mexican and international beers is on the second floor along the water with a terrace ideal for sunsets, a bite to eat and lots of options for the beer lover. Easily the largest selection of beer on the island.
- **El Palomar,** on the corner of Rafael Melgar and 10, is one of the oldest buildings on the island, with a front porch looking out over the water, reminiscent of Hemmingway and a classic tropical sunset. The food is amazing, and their cocktail selection is wide and all handmade. This is quite literally a historic Cozumel experience in a building nearly 100 years old.

**Other options:*

• **The Money Bar**	• **Hemmingway's**	• **Buccanos**
• **Rock 'N Java**	• **No Name Bar**	• **Playa Corona**
• **Guidos**	• **La Monina**	• **Sky Reef**

POOL TABLE ANYONE?

The Green House Bar and Grill $$

A truly unique Cozumel destination, and a haven for 100% Cuban cigars, a humidor with a large selection, new outdoor gardens and patios to enjoy your smoke, delicious food and drinks, and 2 pool tables where the islands best pool sharks gather daily. Sort of a mix Chicago bar and Havana, with stuffed sandwiches like the Lemon Garlic Chicken Sandwich, corned beef, a marvelous shrimp sandwich, excellent burgers, and chicken wings, or classic slow cooked Cuban pork sandwiches.

If you are a pool shark and need a fix, this is your place for sure. Always friendly and welcoming, they even have dartboards and seating inside or out. It does NOT smell like Cigars in here actually if anyone is easily offended, they have taken care of that with a first-rate filtration system that works amazingly well! One of the islands only source for REAL Cuban cigars. They also own a small shop inside Wet Wendy's with the same excellent selection of Cuban's.

Phone: 52-987-103-5726

(On 2, just off Rafael Melgar)

Punta Morena Beach Bar

On the completely other side of the island, at this beach bar, they have a pool table. I wouldn't remotely compare this to the Green House as it's more of a kids table, but whatever, if the urge gets you, do it.

Phone: 52-987-876-1225

(3/4 of the way down the east side from the southern end, impossible to miss)

HOT SPOTS FOR A BEACH VOLLEYBALL GAME

So, there are a few as you might imagine, though some are more consistent than others. I'll begin with a few that always have nets up, and plenty of people playing, OR to recruit, and a few others that are great spots for a pickup beach volleyball game, but don't always seem to have nets up. A lot of that depends on the high season.

Alberto's Beach Bar & Grill

Mentioned earlier in these pages, this great island beach bar always has nets up and eager participants ready for a lively beach volleyball game.

Phone: 52-987-876-1394

Punta Morena Beach Bar

On the islands east side, Punta Morena is always busy on the weekends, and nearly always has nets set up for a game with locals and tourists alike. The sand and beach are beautiful, as are the food and drink.

Phone: 52-987-876-1225

(3/4 of the way down the east side from the southern end, impossible to miss)

Carlos and Charlies Beach Bar

Great sand and lots of good company for a beach volleyball game daily!

Chen Rio Beach

One of the prettiest beaches and quiet coves on the island's east side often has nets set up, particularly on the weekends, and during the busy season December – April

Playa San Martin

The east side's longest continual beach and easily the widest, has volleyball nets up, especially on weekends and during high season.

BEST SPOTS FOR YOUR FAVORITE SPORTS ON TELEVISION

Kelley's Sports Bar $$

For years Kelley's has respected the sports fan and will turn off the music for your favorite Packer, Lakers, Daytona Race, or god forbid a Bears game! Plenty of televisions under an intimate palapa bar in Cozumel's downtown, with excellent sandwiches, burgers, and shots of good tequila if your team is winning!

Phone: 52-987-878-4738

(On 10, between Salas and 1)

Dick's Dive $$

A wonderful spot off the pedestrian walk just north of the square for a game of any kind on television. The ONLY problem here is that often they will not turn off the loud music if you want to enjoy your game. Good food, friendly staff, and excellent service.

(Just north of the square along the pedestrian walk)

Woody's $$

Just around the corner from Dick's, also on the pedestrian walk off the northeast corner of the square, Woody's offers all the games on television, but again, you are often competing with live music to try and listen to your game. Burgers, great cocktails, and a fun island vibe.

(Just east of the Seven–11 on the pedestrian walk off the northeast corner of the square)

Hooters $$

Yes, the same Hooters you know from the states is proudly represented here in Cozumel as part of the Punta Langosta cruise ship pier just south of town. Excellent

Hooters burgers, chicken wings with lots of signature sauces, darn good Bloody Marys, and a fine venue for sports on television when visiting the island.

Phone: 52-987-869-1465

(Punta Langosta cruise pier complex)

No Name Sports Bar $$$

Just south of Punta Langosta cruise ship pier, along the water is No Name, and while not a dedicated sports bar by any means, they are pretty good at keeping the loud music down for a Sunday football game, or any other event if you simply ask. They have 2–3 TVs, good sound, and not a big place, but have a burger and watch your game, and after, jump in the pool and have a cold one along the waterfront or watch a lovely sunset.

Phone: 52-987-878-4020

(Just south of Punta Langosta)

Golfing, Cozumel Country Club

Soon to celebrate their 20th anniversary, Cozumel's lone golf course is located at the end of the north road, 5 miles or so north of town. Designed by Nicklaus Design Group, the course was carefully carved from the island's mangrove choked northern jungles in 2001. Peaceful and quiet, this fine golf course is extremely challenging for the scratch or low handicap golfer, and an awful lot of fun for the novice who will need to have plenty of balls in his or her bag. At Cozumel Country Club you will find all the amenities of any other good golf course, from their complete pro shop to the carefully tended practice greens. The pretty thatched-roof clubhouse has an especially nice spot outdoors to sit and have a drink or a bite to eat, even for the non-golfer. You should be sure to bring plenty of balls along with you because the water features are numerous throughout, and there are several long marshes to clear. Once you crank a ball into the jungle, which you will, don't even consider trying to get your ball back once you shank it here; it's gone! The pro shop has plenty of quality clubs to rent for the day. Rates range from $85.00-$130.00 for 18 holes, with a cart and a couple of cold waters, depending on the time of day and the season.

The first Mexican golf course designated as a Certified Audubon Cooperative Sanctuary, the bird-life is amazing, and the course offers walking tours with local bird experts.

Parque Ecologico Punta Sur (Punta Sur Eco Park)

Established by Presidential Decree back in 1996 as a natural protected area, the park encompasses a large area of land that makes up the southern tip of the island. Punta Sur is designed to protect the existing lagoon community, the coastal dunes, and beaches which support breeding grounds for green and loggerhead sea turtles, and an ecosystem which supports many varieties of animal life including the indigenous crocodile, Roseate spoonbills, wild boar, anteater, flamingoes, a variety of other magnificent bird-life (especially November-March), and the occasional deer.

Currently, the entrance fee is around $14.00 US for the day, but the cost is well worth it! There are 3 separate large lagoons with wooden walkways, viewing towers and at the end of the road, visitors have the opportunity to tour one of the lagoons by boat where the 40-minute ride is led by a guide who discusses the aspects of lagoon life, and you will almost certainly see a large crocodile or two, and colorful bird-life. Sometimes there is a minimal charge of 30 pesos for the boat tour, but often there is no charge. There are also a couple of beach bars, with snorkel gear to rent, food and drink, and lots of free lounge chairs, along with one of the island's best beaches and calm, safe swimming. The snorkeling is quite good, though to reach the area it is a minute or so swim .

Explore the lighthouse and the stunning views from the top. The small nautical museum featuring the history of the island at the base of the lighthouse is reason enough to visit Punta Sur. You will be amazed at what occurred on Cozumel in the past centuries, and its significance to the trade routes of the Caribbean.

Museo De La Cozumel (Cozumel Museum)

After two long years of renovation and remodeling, the island museum has opened once again in late February of 2020! In the same location as it was for years, the improvements according to reports are sensational. Video interaction with many displays, a history of some of the island's oldest restaurants such as Casa Denis, displays explaining the indigenous beginning of the island, the arrival of the Spanish, and even a display of some of the islands local and current artists. As before, the Cozumel Museum was a must-visit for all travelers, and locals, and today that reputation has been vastly improved. Take the time to wander one of the island's humble treasures and discover the magic and history of Cozumel.

Phone: 52-987-872-1522
(Rafael Melgar, between 4 & 6)

Cozumel's Stunning and Remote East Side

There are very few Caribbean landscapes as naturally beautiful as the east coast of Cozumel. While there are some 30 miles of beach and rocky shore, only about 12 miles of it are paved road (2 side by side paved roads right along the coast). The balance of the island is reached by extremely rough sand roads where it is highly advised to never take a rental car (you will get stuck and your insurance will be void), though tours of these parts of the island are available by boat and dune buggy, and we will discuss this later. The old road is now reserved exclusively for cyclists and pedestrians, and only the new road is available for vehicle traffic. Please obey all signs and the blocked access to the cyclist only road, you will be ticketed if driving a vehicle. Access to this side of the island is available by 2 routes only from the other side of the island. In town, if you follow Avenue Benito Juarez east, it turns into the transversal road and it will take you 11 miles east to the iconic Mezcalito's Restaurant on the east side of the island, where the paved road then turns south and goes all the way to Punta Sur Park. Your other option is to follow the main west coast road (Ave. Rafael Melgar) south from town, pass the cruise ship piers and drive the 20 odd miles to Punta Sur Park on the island's southern tip, where the paved road then heads north and ends at Mezcalito's. Either way is fine, though if returning along the west coast side option, leave early because traffic can be very congested as you reach the town and the cruise ship piers by 3:30 p.m.

Be prepared when traveling to this side as there is no electricity and rare cell phone reception. All the small beach bars are run by generators and are only open roughly from 10:00 a.m.–5:00 p.m. daily. The food is wonderful and the drinks flow at each of the small destinations over here. Swimming is certainly tempting, though be very careful as rip tides and undertows can be dangerous. For the swimmer, I would restrict myself to Playa San Martin, and the calmer coves of Punta Morena and Playa Chiqueros (near El Pescador Restaurant), and then only if the "safe" green flags are up denoting safe swimming conditions. Also, if swimming is your objective, find yourself at the stunning beach inside Punta Sur Park. The beach at the end of the park road is beautiful and nearly always with conditions conducive to safe swimming.

Rastas Beach Bar, Welcome to Miami, San Martin Beach, Coconuts, Señor Iguanas, Punta Morena, and Mezcalitos all provide the visitor with delightful cocktails, gorgeous views, and wonderful food. For the adventurous looking for a starlit night on the east side, Hotel Ventanas Al Mar is the only hotel on that side of the island, and an evening there is something special. Sixteen rooms, a heart-shaped pool, and peace and quiet every night.

While swimming at the east side beaches can be questionable at times, the walker, runner, cyclist, sun worshiper, nature lover, stone collector, photographer or love makers, will find endless sand, and secret nooks with which to explore. If you choose to spend your day this way or even a few hours, be sure to bring along plenty of sunscreen, bottled water, beach blankets, and towels. Even if you are not the adventurous type, rent a car or catch a taxi to see this beautiful side of the island.

San Gervasio Ruins

The island is teeming with un-excavated ruins, generally small, but the deep jungles of the island are filled with mystery and intrigue, mostly still in private hands. San Gervasio Archaeological Zone is the only publicly accessible and partially excavated large site of the ancient Mayan people on the island. It is said to have been the center of pilgrimages on the island, for the Mayan people to worship the goddess Ixchel (goddess of love and fertility). Historians, archaeologists, and local residents still debate the actual proximity of her temple, as adjacent ruins which are still in private hands, may in fact point to more significant sites where these pilgrimages took place. Nonetheless, San Gervasio is a fascinating step back into the history of this island.

While not comparable to the mainland sites of Ek Balam, Coba, Chichen Itza or Tulum, in size or scope, a visit to San Gervasio is a fascinating step back in time. With 6 separate small sites, and isolated temples and residences, all are connected by an ancient stone path (sacbe), where you will have the chance to follow the worn footsteps of those one thousand years ago. The site dates back to 1000 A.D.-1650 A.D. Plenty of signage and descriptions of the sites enable those who choose to tour the site on their own, but tours are available. Plenty of free parking and an entrance fee of around $7.00 allows you to visit the site for as long as you wish. Bring bug repellent, sunscreen, and good walking shoes, either boots or sneakers, as the terrain and stone paths are rough and uneven. Do not visit in flip flops. You will find plenty of shade in the lush jungle setting, and seating to rest during your hike through the grounds. One to two hours may be enough for most, but take your time as there is much to see and learn. Souvenirs and drinks are available at the entrance. Keep your eyes open as the bird watching can be excellent.

(About 6 miles east of town on the transversal road)

The Mayan Bee Sanctuary

Having opened in 2019, this is a tour and sanctuary unique to Cozumel. Featuring the culture and production of honey from the sting-less Melipona Bee, the site and tour provide a fascinating look into this micro-culture of local honey production in Cozumel and the Yucatan peninsula of Mexico. Melipona Bees, of which there are 100's of species in mostly sub and tropical locations worldwide, are found almost exclusively in Mexico, in the southern Yucatan jungles.

Stingless yes, and while the bees do have small stingers, they are too small to use as a defense mechanism, though the bees will protect their nests by biting. The quality and uses of the honey produced by these bees go back centuries in the Mayan world, and here at The Mayan Bee Sanctuary, you will be introduced to not only the danger these bees face in the modern world, but to the management and preservation of this unique bee, and to the research being done to improve traditional beekeeping techniques.

Samples are available during your visit as are plenty of products to purchase, from honey, skin care products, spa products, and much, much more. Samples of active nests are a part of this interactive tour focusing on the production, importance, and the many health qualities of Melipona honey. There is a store for purchase of products, trails, and displays, and as you tour this place, you will also find stone sculptures and the work of local Cozumel artist, Carlos Francisco Polanco Pacheco. In addition, you will see a beautiful yet small cenote on the property.

(About 8 miles east of town on the transversal road)

The Community of El Cedral (Cozumel's Second Town)

The island of Cozumel is home to only 2 towns, San Miguel the main city, and El Cedral, about 10 miles south of San Miguel on the west coast road. One might refer to El Cedral as the island's "forgotten community," and it is I suppose, but a visit is very interesting. Historically, both communities have a significant and critical history to the development of the island we know today, but little is left in El Cedral, though what remains is worth a visit for sure, if only as an alternate perspective.

South of town, the entrance is impossible to miss, just look for the large arched entrance that says El Cedral! Follow the road past a few ranches, fields and jungle, for maybe a mile, and on your right, you will see one of the cutest police stations ever! Pass the station and park where there is a plaza, tequila tasting, a couple of shops, a lovely little chapel adjacent to a small ruin, and explore a bit. If the shopping and tequila tasting doesn't intrigue you, at least check out the chapel, then wander the streets in town, you will see some of the island's prettiest little homes and gardens. The community here is quiet and quaint. I have been known to drive in and just spend an hour walking the streets and admiring what could be a wonderful little spot to retire someday, it is quite charming.

(About 10 miles south of town on the west coast road)

Rancho Buenavista/Hidden Mayan Trails

For 6 decades or so, the Villanueva family has owned and operated this very cool island ranch. Located just off the east coast road, feel free to drive in (except Sundays) and take a look. Over 100 years ago the ranch operated as a pineapple and sugarcane farm where the products were exported to the outside world. The Villanueva family has operated the ranch for many years as a haven for horseback riding and exploring the nearly 500 acres of jungle, lagoons, caves, and Post Classic Maya ruins. The lagoons feature some of the most remarkable birding opportunities on the island. Flamingoes, Ibis, Roseate spoonbill, Herons, Egrets, and many more species are easily seen.

Today, horseback riding through the ranch remains, but mountain bike trails and tours are now available through the property, as are birding tours.

(Contact Bruno Villanueva at www.hiddenmayantrails.com)
(A couple of miles north of Punta Sur on the east coast road)

Parque Benito Juarez (Benito Juarez Park)

Named after former President Benito Juarez (1858–1872), President Juarez is remembered nationwide as a symbol of Mexican nationalism and for his resistance to foreign intervention. The park named after him in Cozumel is sort of the entrance point for many to the island. Adjacent to the ferry pier for Playa Del Carmen and the mainland, Benito Juarez Park has fountains, benches, murals, many shops, shade trees, a clock tower, restaurants lining the pedestrian walks and numerous kiosks with countless items available for purchase. In the evenings, the park transforms into a haven for families and children after a long day, playing in the splash fountain, wandering the paths, and conversing on the many park benches. Food carts arrive in the evenings with tacos, ice cream, churro desserts, and much more. Many nights, the park is a host to live music, dance, opera, symphony music, and other live entertainment.

In many ways, this is the heart of the island from where all adventure begins, or where you can people watch and plan your day, or breathe in the fresh tropical evening air after a long day. Steps away from the waterfront, enjoy a magnificent island sunset within the pulse of Cozumel.

CHURCHES/CHAPELS, AND THE COZUMEL CEMETERY

The island is home to several lovely churches and cemeteries, we will mention a few of significance.

San Miguel Church

(Iglesia de San Miguel) is the main, most well-known, and maybe the most photographed church on the island. Masses are available in Spanish and English.

(On the corner of 10 and the northeast pedestrian walk, a block east of the town square)

The Cathedral of Corpus Christi

(Iglesia Corpus Christi) is also a widely photographed and beautiful architectural gem on the island.
(Corner of 15 and 70)

Stella Maris Chapel (Capilla Stella Maris)

Maybe the most charming and beautiful small chapel on the island. Located right on the water, next to the Sky Reef Beach Club, the interwoven natural woodwork here, and the open setting are absolutely stunning in the simplest of ways. If I were to get married on Cozumel, this would easily be my number one choice! I have a friend on the island who has lived there 25 years, and she had never seen it, or maybe had just passed it by. It is one of those tiny spots that when on the old road south of town in search of something, you could conceivably just pass it by.
(A couple of miles south of the last cruise ship pier, next to Sky Reef)

Capilla Santa Cruz De Cuzamil (Santa Cruz Chapel of Cozumel)

Nearly completed in early 2020, as a commemoration to the first mass on the island 500 years ago, and the first masses original proximity on the island (in fact it is believed to have been in another location, but whatever), it is gorgeous! North of the Playa ferry pier and built in the boulevard separating the north and southbound lanes of Rafael

Melgar right before the airport road. The newest church on the island and it is simply stunning.

The Cozumel Cemetery

This may seem like an odd suggestion, but it is quite interesting to stroll through and pay respect to many that have lived here and helped build Cozumel into what it is today. Some of the oldest and most influential families are interred here, and it is a colorful example of local tradition and of the respect given to those who have passed. Look for the large iron gate and feel free to respectfully wander through this interesting piece of island history.

(On 5 ave. sur, just south of calle 9 at the turn in the road)

A FUN COZUMEL SCAVENGER HUNT!

This is a compilation of many that I have put together over the years. A scavenger hunt is perfect for families, wedding parties, or any group excursion to the island. They are great fun at the very least, but along with this book, it is an excellent way to quickly become familiar with the island and many of its hidden secrets you otherwise may not be inspired to discover.

Your objective is to find as many of the following items or scenarios as possible. A digital picture or the object as deemed appropriate is proof of your find. Please do not disturb the environment or trespass as you go through your hunt unless it is to pick up litter. You set the time limit, some of this stuff is tough.

Let the games begin!

- A Picture of you with a fresh tortilla purchased from Genesis Tortileria, including a pic of their sign as proof .... 10 pts.
- One piece of sea glass .... 10 pts.
- A picture of a golf cart at Cozumel Country Club .... 5 pts.
- A picture of a freshly caught fish .... 10 pts.
- A Superior beer cap or a bottle of Superior beer .... 5 pts.
- One seashell .... 5 pts.
- An entry stub from San Gervasio Ruins .... 5 pts.
- A picture of an iguana 10 pts. *15 pts. If it is missing a part of its tail!
- A picture of Chapel Stella Maris near Sky Reef .... 10pts.
- A picture of a frigate bird aloft .... 15 pts.
- An Indio beer label .... 5 pts.
- A ferry receipt from Playa Del Carmen .... 10 pts.
- A picture of a pelican .... 5 pts.
- A small bit of seaweed .... 5 pts.
- A picture of you under the water at the town squares splash fountain .... 15 pts.
- A picture of anything besides a human eating a piece of coconut .... 15 pts.
- A picture of you in a cave .... 25 pts.
- 1 coconut shell .... 5 pts.
- 1 dried palm frond picked up from the ground .... 10 pts.
- 1 bird feather .... 5 pts.
- 1 plastic, empty bottle found during your hunt, make it 2 or more and appropriately throw it out later .... 1 pt. per bottle!
- A picture of any sculpture .... 5 pts.
- A picture of a jet ski .... 10 pts.
- A picture of any Cerveceria Punta Sur made beer .... 10 pts.

- A picture of Nacho from Cozumel Surfing   15 pts.
- A picture of someone with a cocktail in a coconut shell   15 pts.
- A picture of the Galeria Azul sign   15 pts.
- A picture of anyone playing checkers with bottle caps   20 pts.
- A picture of a chair at Mueblos Rusticos   15 pts.
- A picture of someone cooking Tix 'N Chic   15 pts.
- A picture of local kids playing soccer   10 pts.
- A picture of either the red, yellow or green safety flags at a beach   10 pts.
- A picture of fishing nets drying   15 pts.
- A picture of a Bimbo dog stand   10 pts.
- A picture of you in a snorkel, mask, and fins   15 pts.
- A picture of the Casa Denis Restaurant sign   10 pts.
- A picture of any sign saying Temazcal   15 pts.
- A picture of the new church in the boulevard north of the ferry pier   5 pts.
- A picture of a jar of honey at the Maya Bee Sanctuary   10 pts.
- A picture of a lighthouse   10 pts.
- A picture of a local crocodile   15 pts.
- A picture of a piece of Key Lime Pie   10 pts.
- A picture of a hammock between 2 trees   10 pts.
- A picture of anyone playing the guitar, with a ponytail   15 pts.
- A picture of anyone sitting at a swim-up bar   10 pts.
- A picture of a sign with Bob Marley's photo on it   10 pts.

Bonus Questions:

- Any picture of someone on a tandem bicycle   50 pts.
- A picture of a mural with a fish on it   25 pts.
- A photo of someone on a Harley Davidson   75 pts.

Good luck and have a blast!

BEST SHOPPING FOR ALL

For shopping, you can essentially break Cozumel down into 3 specific locations. For those arriving via cruise ship, there are the pedestrian malls at Punta Langosta nearest to town, or the mall at Puerta Maya and the International Pier (within a 1,000 feet of each other and 4 miles south of town), and finally, the plaza of Benito Juarez Park and the streets of San Miguel town itself. In San Miguel, you will find the best variety and the largest assortment of shopping venues, whether it is one of the large tourist one-stop shops or one of the many fun local shops. The following selections cover it all and will widen your scope when visiting the island. As you explore, you will find more!

Punta Langosta

The cruise ship pier closest to town by only a matter of blocks, has all the international flavors and restaurants from Hooters, to Señor Frogs, and a maze of international shopping with a couple of dozen shops featuring everything from T-shirts to hammocks, tiny souvenir shops or the much larger Del Sol, Sunglass Hut, Cariloha, and others. Like anywhere down here, many of the smaller shops will have hawkers trying to get you inside and if you are not interested, keep walking and give them a polite "no thank you." It may take two "no thank you's," but this simple response is the best way to get the point across that you are not interested. Any shop without hawkers out front may be a better choice anyway.

Puerta Maya and the International Pier

One expansive mall serves both cruise ship piers (actually one at the International pier and two piers at Puerta Maya). Similar to Punta Langosta, but more expansive, you will find several international dining options such as Fat Tuesday, or a more local option like Cozumel's own Panchos Backyard. Shopping here at the mall includes several dozen shops arranged in pleasant surroundings where one could if they wished to spend the entire day. Shopping includes amongst others, the Yucatan's very own Los Cinco Soles (maybe the most amazing store on the island, which I believe has 3 locations, plus more on the mainland), Piranha Joes, Zingara Swimwear, Hammock Island, Le Best, Viva Mexico, and many others. I encourage you, shoppers, to enjoy the options here, especially if you are visiting by ship for the day, otherwise, get yourself 4 -5 miles north to San Miguel town and wander the streets for some unique shopping.

(4–5 miles south of town on the main west coast road)

FINEST JEWELRY

Sergios Silver from Taxco $$-$$$

The silver products here are among the finest, if not the finest on the island. Whether you purchase one of the many stock items or have a piece custom made, the options for the silver connoisseur are limitless at this low pressure and high-quality island shop. The selection of bracelets or cuffs, for men and women, feature designs fitting for any shopper. Silver, with turquoise or abalone pendants and brooches, silver necklaces, bracelets, rings, and earrings are all available.

(At the southeast corner the main plaza in town, right next to Woody's)

Déjà Vu Leather and Jewelry $$-$$$

A small island shop owned by an incredibly talented jeweler, artist, designer, and craftsman of both silver, gem, and leather products. Antonio has been here for years and is the go-to designer for jewelry and leather for many return visitors yearly, and Cozumel residents. Whether it is to repair watches, earrings or bracelets, or mend your leather purse, his skill and workmanship are second to none. Your experience here will be low pressure, and any questions will be answered with as much detail as you need. Stock designs or custom made, jewelry, gems, or dress and casual leather sandals, purses, belts, dress shoes, and even hats. A must stop on this island for the discerning shopper.

(Rafael Melgar just south of calle 9, on the ocean side)

Los Cinco Soles $$-$$$

As they say at Los Cinco Soles, "All of Mexico Under One Roof". That statement may best describe the variety of excellence one will find at this long time Cozumel shop. There are I believe 3 locations on the island and several on the mainland, including the Cancun airport. Jewelry aside, the selections here of products created by families, artisans, and farmers throughout the country, are all the finest quality.

Arts and Crafts, boutique clothing, pure vanilla, cookware, table clothes, home décor, art, Mexican spices and ingredients, coffee, Talavera work, wall art, and pottery, a huge selection of tequila and mezcal, and of course jewelry. Their jewelry is brought in from all over Mexico from buyers who understand and know the artisans. Silver jewelry from workshops in Taxco and Guanajuato, Mexican beadwork from Puebla, glass fusion pieces from Merida, and ceramic, clay, papier mache, and metal designs from jewelry artisans of Jalisco state. Los Cinco Soles is easily the most complete and representative shop on the island of handmade Mexican products since 1984.

Phone: 52-987-872-9004
(Rafael Melgar on the corner with 8)

I Love Mexico $$

You will love your stop at this fun little shop just off the main square owned by a delightfully creative and friendly couple. A quiet vibe fills this small place of unique gifts not found anywhere else on the island. Much of the jewelry is displayed by the stone used, from opals to ambers, as well as sterling silver pieces of the highest quality. Purses, bags, folk art, Christmas ornaments, painted wooden earrings, and wall hangings, all uniquely designed, are available from this lovely island store.

(On the pedestrian walk just south of the town square)

LOCAL ART/SHOPS

Aside from those mentioned above, the following local stores offer some of the island's most unique and fun shopping.

Los Cinco Soles $$-$$$

Yes, we just mentioned this great shop, but to reiterate, here is where you will find the best and the highest quality of a universe of handmade Mexican products.

Phone: 52-987-872-9004
(Rafael Melgar on the corner with 8)

Galeria Azul $$

An institution on the island owned by two local artists who create some of the most unique and stunning work anywhere. Greg and Liliana operate this studio and workshop in front of their island home. Greg Dietrich's hand-blown lamps, glass vessels, and etched glass are simply beautiful and one-of-a-kind. His work blends his skill as a glassblower with his love of the Cozumel world around him, in particular marine life. Only Greg himself can describe this remarkable work best, so visit his website where you will see samples and videos of how these pieces are made, it is a long and tedious process.

His wife Liliana Macotela is an equally talented and award-winning photographer and artist in her own right. Her striking black and white photography is in a class of its own, both mesmerizing and thought-provoking, each photograph is a story. Liliana and Greg are ambassadors and promoters of local art and education on the island. Visit their shop Monday-Friday, from 11:00 a.m.–7:00 p.m., or by appointment. For a mix of

fine art and local culture, feel free to stop in and browse and purchase. You will get an education here for sure.

Phone: 52-987-869-0963

(On 15, between 8 & 10)

Muebles Rusticos (Rustic Furniture) $-$$$

Cluttered and filled to the rafters, like something magical out of Harry Potter, Muebles Rusticos is the home of hand-carved furniture and brightly colored pottery, Talavera work, wall art, wood carvings, dinnerware, and so very much more fascinating works of art, but it is the furniture here that is the real show-stopper. Cribs, headboards, chairs, desks, practically anything to furnish your home is available here in some of the most unusual and unique designs I have seen anywhere. Back a few blocks from the town square, you rarely hear folks discuss this place, but I stop in every visit, the shop is fascinating!

(On 15, between 2 and Benito Juarez)

Galo Art Studio $-$$

Galo Ramirez and Niurka Guzman are the artists that own and operate this painting studio and shop, a 15-minute walk east of the waterfront. Both artists have won multiple awards locally and internationally, and promote work with many artists throughout the island. They are actively involved in the education of local children and adults on Cozumel with a variety of painting workshops. Galo and Niurka represent art in its purest form, they live and breathe their work and the promotion of others. You will most certainly find something for your home as you browse their work in their tiny island studio.

Phone: 52-987-102-0755

(On Felipe Angeles, between A. R. Salas and 3 sur, just east of Ave. 30)

El Rincon De Addy $-$$

Addy Bacelis displays her genius daily at her small island café and studio, where you will see her most days overseeing the cooks and working with her brush. The food is delicious and presented beautifully as an artist just might, and her work is on both canvas and an array of household items you would never imagine. Not to mention on all the chairs, tables, walls, and hanging discreetly and randomly amongst the branches of massive trees, where customers enjoy the open breeze and natural shade of her island oasis. Look for the brightly painted entrance and step into the amazing life and world of Cozumel artist Addy Bacelis. I heard someone mention upon entering into Addy's place, "Your soul will be at peace." That is exactly right.

Phone: 52-987-872-4198

(On 5, between 30 and 25)

Shalom $$

For the most part, this shop is for women, OR to purchase something special for the woman in your life. Their selection of jewelry, women's clothing, swimwear, pillows, purses and handbags, hats, scarves, and earrings is excellent, and much of it is handmade. Almost everything available in this cute little store you have never seen, and will never see again.

(At the southeast corner of the square just a few doors down the pedestrian walk)

Rogers Boots $$

Not really a local shop, it is a chain, but their leather goods and of course boots are of excellent quality. Purses, belts, boots, sandals, dress shoes, wallets, and much more are available at Rogers Boots.

(On Salas, between Rafael Melgar and 5)

The Spice and Tea Market $$

Dozens of authentic Mexican sauces and salsas from a spicy peanut salsa, to their mole sauces and a chipotle pepper salsa, are only the beginning of what you will find here. Either for your own cooking purposes on the island, or a nice package to return home with or as a gift, the spice and tea selections here are incredible. Hibiscus teas, pure vanilla, a lemonade mix with lemongrass, cranberry, raisins and hibiscus, homemade guacamole seasonings, smoked chipotle, a wide array of herbal teas, soaps, cocoa mixes, fresh and organic spices of all kinds and soup mixes, are all available at Cozumel's premier spice market.

Phone: 52-987-872-0273

(Rafael Melgar, between 2 & 4)

Puro Relajo

Bring the family and the kids to this incredible party shop on the island. Nope, not tequila, but rather here you will find an amazing supply of party goods for nearly any occasion. A large assortment of pinatas hanging from the ceilings, an assortment of thousands of candies from all over Mexico, games, party plates, napkins, and nearly anything else you could possibly want for a birthday, graduation, anniversary or any type of island party.

Phone: 52-987-871-9055

(Ave. 30, between 3 and Morelos)

Mercado Municipal (Municipal Market) $

The municipal market buzzes all day (particularly mornings and early afternoons) with fresh fish, vegetables, fruits, fresh tortillas and clothing, sometimes hammocks, and lots of other fun goods to browse away the day in Cozumel's premier open-air local market. There are several local restaurants as well to enjoy some island cuisine.
(Corner of A. R. Salas and 20)

The Fisherman's Co-op $

Come here typically in the mornings, and you will have the opportunity to purchase fresh fish by weight almost literally right off the boat, or close to it!
(Ave. 5, right past 9 before you reach the cemetery)

Floreria Evelyn $

A flower shop filled with fresh flowers either by arrangement, or loose for you to select from. The smells and selection are excellent, and the ladies will help you select what you need.
(Calle 1 and 25)

Floreria La Riviera

Literally across the street from the above, and I have no idea if they are owned by the same people, but the flower selections are equally as fresh and beautiful.
Phone: 52-984-206-1717
(Calle 1 and 25)

CHOICE CIGARS

Cigars can be found everywhere on the island, though if you are looking for a treat, a Cuban cigar, there are only three spots on the island where you can be assured of the real thing.

The Green House Cigar Bar

Pool tables, darts, a back outdoor patio, and lots of fun at this combination Chicago pool hall and Havana bar. A true haven for real Cubans and a comfortable place to smoke one!
Phone: 52-987-103-5726
(On 2, between Rafael Melgar and 5)

Havana Bobs Cuban Cigars $$

In the Wet Wendy's complex, the same man who owns The Green House operates a cigar store featuring a walk-in humidor and the best in Cuban cigars. Open Monday-Saturday, 10:30–4:00 p.m. and 7:00–10:00 p.m.
(Just walk north a half block from the town square and you will see it on the pedestrian walk)

La Casa Del Mojito $$

Delicious Cuban pulled pork sandwiches, a selection of wonderful mojitos and Cuban cigar specials. A small restaurant and bar with real Cubans.
(On 5, between A. R. Salas and 3)

BEST TEQUILA SELECTIONS

Los Cinco Soles $$-$$$

Even the non-shopper could spend a good amount of time in this wonderful store downtown. The selection of tequila will not disappoint, there are several hundred varieties available. Ask for a sample.

Phone: 52-987-872-9004

(Rafael Melgar on the corner with 8)

Mega Market $$

Having revolutionized shopping on the island back in 2008 when this supermarket first opened, it is taken for granted these days. Yes, the tequila selection is particularly good, as is everything a modern supermarket should be. Bread, cheeses, a full deli, meats, seafood, fruits and veggies, appliances, TVs, bikes, beach toys, a full pharmacy, clothing, and pretty much everything else, you get the picture. Great wine selection as well.

(On the oceanfront road just south of town between 11 & 13)

Chedraui $$

Remarkably similar to Mega above, and right next door, with pretty much all the same things and also a nice selection of tequila! They have just opened a new location on the transversal road east of town. I believe the new one is at the first roundabout. Also, with a good wine selection.

(On the oceanfront road just south of town between 11 & 13)

Cava Del Duero $

A small liquor store but always with excellent prices and a good selection of tequila. This is usually my place to purchase booze when visiting Cozumel. It used to be called Covi, so do not be confused.

Phone: 52-987-872-5574

(NW corner of 30 and 2)

La Europea $$

Relatively new to the island (since 2014), La Europea is sort of a specialty shop featuring wine, liquor and gourmet deli products. The selection isn't huge, but it is select products of the best quality. The tequila and wine selections are outstanding.

(Rafael Melgar between 9 & 11)

Tequila Town $$

Tequila, mezcal, and lots of it.

(NE corner of 5 and A. R. Salas)

"There are no people who are quite so vulgar as the over-refined".

Mark Twain

SUPERMARKETS AND CONVENIENCE STORES

I won't go into much detail at all here, as most of what you need to know was just mentioned. Convenience stores are all over the island, just look for "SIX" or "OXXO," they are everywhere and carry your typical convenience store stuff from soda, beer, snacks, crackers, lighters, etc. There is also a 7–Eleven of all things right on the northeast corner of the square in town. I will mention that here there are a handful of additional stores/markets that just may come in handy for you.

Soriana's Market $

More used by locals, and it is still an excellent store, though you won't find the selection of a Mega or Chedraui. Soriana's is a perfectly fine choice unless you need some specialty item, they essentially have everything else.

(Ave. 30 on the corner with 4)

Super AKI $

Similar to Soriana's above, maybe a little larger and a tad more selection, but the two are very comparable.

Phone: 52-987-872-1710

(Ave. 30 and Juarez)

Pacsa Deli $$

Unless you live here, most likely you will have no need for this excellent and out of the way deli, but it is one of Cozumel's best! Often when shopping for some specialty items, it can be a crapshoot as to where to find it between the markets on the island. I can't tell you how often I hear from expat locals, "Well I saw it at Pacsa Deli." Aside from being a wonderful full deli with cheeses and meats, it is a spice haven! Specialty desserts, Thai sauces and pastes, tahini, tofu, peanut oil, garam masala, pumpkin puree, brown sugar, an array of salsas, soy and veggie burgers, apple cider vinegar, vegan products, chocolates and lots more! Honestly, 20 years ago nobody even blinked an eye or considered needing any of this when visiting Cozumel. Times have changed!

Phone: 52-987-869-1935

(East of town on 2 between 45 and 50)

TOURISTY/SOUVENIR SHOPPING

The following section is probably more for those of you here maybe for a day, or if you have had a long week and need to do some quick shopping for the kids or friends at home, souvenir stuff! This will include not only a couple of individual shops but also particularly pretty areas to browse with multiple shops. So, don your most comfortable sandals and have fun exploring.

Confetti Street

Within view of the town square, this lovely side street is a great place to stroll and browse. As of yet though, the shops don't approach the quality of the atmosphere. You may very well see something you like so don't get me wrong, but I've always thought it best as a place for taking a great picture or enjoying a short and peaceful walk off the main drag, with the sounds of birds singing from above.

(Directly off the pedestrian walk along the southwest edge of the town square)

Villa Mar $$

This tastefully designed and often busy pedestrian shopping area encompasses your classic touristy shops filled with mostly typical souvenirs. Shops change here often, but with its attractive and gallery-like atmosphere, the only thing it lacks is the gallery. If there is a place in downtown San Miguel that screams out, "Put some cool shops in here." This would be it. This is still an area you will want to explore because it is pretty and you never know if someone has opened up something that might encourage Villa Mar to live up to its potential.

(Just off the NW corner of the town square)

Hotel Vista Del Mar $$

Not part of the hotel itself, but come in off the main drag through the arched entrance and you will find all kinds of small shops filled with T-shirts, hammocks, women's wraps, beach accessories, mostly factory-made Mexican souvenirs, and much more. The shopping area is a ½ block long with perhaps 15 little stall type shops where the ardent shopper could fill endless bags with all sorts of fun, simple things for those waiting at home. The atmosphere is shaded and pleasant enough, and usually busy, and it fairly resembles an old-world Mexican market.

Phone: 52-987-872-0545
(Rafael Melgar, between calle 5 & 7)

Viva Mexico $$

A good spot for last-minute shopping that is not cheap, or high end. The selection of liquor isn't bad, as are some of the medium range cigars, but they have a nice selection of clothing, T-shirts, wraps, shorts, swimwear, picture frames, and tons of other basic souvenirs. Upstairs you will find some attractive serving trays, housewares, wall art, Talavera work, and much more. Food is available for dining and live music at night. Viva Mexico is a great spot for a beautiful Cozumel sunset!

(Ave Rafael Melgar and A. R. Salas)

SCUBA DIVING IN COZUMEL

Let me preface this by saying I am not a diver, snorkeling yes. I have snorkeled (in the past 45 years) from Kenya to Egypt, Belize, and most of the Yucatan coastline, including nearly all of Cozumel's, Isla Mujeres and Isla Contoy's shallow reef system, most of which are unfortunately either gone or badly damaged today. I was fortunate to have seen the shallow reefs off Akumal, Isla Mujeres, and Cozumel when they were vibrant and stunning, and while those days are in the past, there is still some decent shore access snorkeling to be found off Cozumel. That will be discussed a bit later.

The spectacular and easily accessible reef system which makes Cozumel a world-class dive destination is part of the second-largest barrier reef in the world, second in size to only the Great Barrier Reef off Australia. This vast system begins 70 miles north of Cozumel at Isla Contoy and stretches south several hundred miles into the waters off Honduras in Central America.

Cozumel's reef systems offer the diver an amazing variety of depth, coral and marine life, which have been attracting divers from all over the world for the better part of 70 years! Divers can explore any of the 8 major reef systems that are easily within reach of the island. Each offers spectacular underwater scenery with varying depths and many different varieties of coral, fish, and an infinite amount of underwater life. From the unique coral mounds of Chankanaab to the great wall dive of Santa Rosa, or experience Paraiso Bajo, Columbia, Yucab, San Francisco, Paso Del Cedral, or what so astounded Cousteau, the coral mountain of Palancar Reef. These sites are all on the west side of the island. The east side offers some outstanding diving as well, though it is far less traveled due to conditions needing to be safe on the windward side. Punta Molas, Hanan, and El Islote are a sampling of the east coast sites.

You will find caves and tunnels of all shapes and sizes in these waters, sponges of all kinds, black coral trees, huge grouper, manta rays, brain coral, cactus coral, moray eel, sea horses, and so much more. The professional dive outfits and guides throughout the island will be your passport to experiencing some of the most diverse scuba diving in the world, and to the unique drift diving revolutionized in Cozumel to safely navigate the islands strong currents when diving.

EXCEPTIONAL DIVE/SNORKEL SHOPS AND GUIDES

Many fine dive operators have worked out of Cozumel for years. When choosing one though, it is highly recommended that you contact them either through e-mail or

phone prior to your arrival on the island. The quality of service, experience, and equipment available can vary greatly. Price should not be a factor when considering a dive operator, safety and experience should come first; your life will be in their hands. Whether you only want to get out to the reef for a snorkel, or a full dive, there are many decisions to be made as to which guide on the island you choose to use.

As I said, price should by no means be a deciding factor, and you will first want to verify that your operator is either PADI or NAUI certified at the very least. Make sure the operator you choose will carry all the necessary safety equipment, including enough life jackets, a radio, and oxygen. What kind of shape the boats are in can tell you a lot about the guide you choose. Do they provide computer diving? Ask how many others will be on the boat and in the water with you, and is the operator's dive protocol what you are most comfortable with. Most importantly, are they pushy or are they considerate, do they take the time to answer your questions, and do they look you in the eye when speaking with you? Feel free to interview them in your own way, there ought to be no rush. While you should be able to meet the owner or one of the managers, often during the busy season this can be difficult. But if you can, their demeanor will be a good gauge as to how you will be treated by the rest of the staff.

The following dive shops recommended are only a sample, but they are considered some of the best and most experienced on the island. There are plenty of others who are outstanding as well. Choose carefully and take your time, but most importantly enjoy one of the world's premier dive destinations comfortably and safely.

Deep Blue Dive Center

Deep Blue is one of the best-equipped, and its staff some of the most experienced and knowledgeable on the island. They have been PADI, NAUI and IANTD certified since 1995. The maximum per boat is 6–8, and all divers will be placed in boats according to experience. They offer a complete line of first-rate rental equipment. Deep Blue is a safety-first operation.

Phone: 52-987-118-2639

(On 10 ave. sur and A. R. Salas)

Eagle Ray Divers

A long time Cozumel dive operator since 1991. Eagle Ray will customize any trip for you, whether you are planning on diving or snorkeling. The owners and staff are patient with all levels and experience of their clientele, including families. Numbers are kept to a minimum on their boats.

Phone: 52-987-107-2315

Aqua Safari

A dive pioneer and one of the oldest operators on the island for nearly 50 years. Aqua Safari is still clearly one of the best with a fleet of well-maintained boats and a complete selection of rental gear. Depending on the boat, you will be diving with a maximum of 12–16 on their larger boats or with a maximum of 5–8 on their small boats. Their pier is directly across from their shop on Cozumel's main drag, and the guides are excellent. Complete instruction is available from this PADI 5-star IDC facility. Aqua Safari is one of the best.

www.aquasafari.com

(Ave. Rafael Melgar, between 5 & 7)

Scuba Tony

Consistently one of the island's most popular and highly rated dive operators. Scuba Tony features a maximum of 6 divers per boat, calling their service, "concierge diving." Any skill level, including training for beginners. At Scuba Tony, for the past nearly two decades, they pride themselves on excellence and service to their customers.

Phone: 52-987 878-2432

Blue Angel Dive Resort

For many years, Blue Angel's intimate and family-like operation has been introducing guests to the beauty of Cozumel diving. The resort of some 20 rooms is right on the water, quirky and funky, and with consistent professionalism readily apparent to all who come back here year after year. The on-site dive shop is PADI 5 Star rated, rentals are available, as is instruction for any level diver. Typically, boats go out with 8–10 divers. The staff is fun, energetic, organized, and thorough. Blue Angel was mentioned earlier in these pages as the food is excellent and dining is open to the public.

Phone: 52-987-872-0188

(A short mile or so south of the town square on the oceanfront road)

Chili Charters

A small family operation, Chili Charters offers snorkel and dive trips, fishing trips, as well as relaxing and beautiful sunset tours. Their fleet of 4 boats will handle groups as small as 5–6, or larger groups of up to 16–18, depending on whether guests are diving or snorkeling. Book a fishing trip with a small group of friends, or a sunset cruise for a larger group of up to 25.

Phone: 52-987-117-4819

Scuba with Alison

Intimate and personalized diving at its best. An NAUI and PADI master instructor, Alison brings nearly 30 years of experience and a philosophy of personal service, customizing each dive with each diver, or small groups, offering lots of flexibility. Her trips have a maximum of 8 divers.

Phone: 52-987-878-5071

Aldora Divers

Specializing in small groups of 6 or less, Aldora Divers has been serving Cozumel divers since 1995. What sets them apart somewhat is their experience in rarely explored sites such as the windward (east coast) of Cozumel where the reefs are brilliant, but conditions are prohibitive much of the time. Aldora will handle all of your diving needs, they are PADI certified and will take you to dive sites others may not.

Phone: 52-987-872-3397

*There are many other outstanding dive shops with years of experience on the island, enjoy your diving!

DIVING AND SNORKEL SUPPLIES

The guides and or dive shops listed above all either have or will arrange for any purchase or rental of equipment. The following are a couple of long-standing places that will cater to any diving supply requirements you could ever need on the island.

Pro Dive

Pro Dive is a premier supply shop for divers and snorkeling enthusiasts of all levels. They offer an excellent selection of fins, masks, dive suits, wet suits, and even a good selection of beach towels and T-shirts. Their staff is knowledgeable and friendly. In addition, they provide underwater camera equipment, computer equipment, weights, cleaning solutions, books on coral and fish ID, waterproof and mesh bags, and just about anything else you might need to make your diving or snorkeling experience the best. The shop features CRESSI dive suits and SCUBA MAX reef boots plus much more. Stop in and see the friendly people at Pro Dive on your next visit to Cozumel.

Phone: 52-984-745-0763

(A.R. Salas and 5)

Cozumel Scuba Repair

Dive equipment storage, repair, cleaning, rental, or purchase of literally all your diving or snorkel gear. The professionals behind this operation represent more years of diving experience, and equipment maintenance than you can imagine, and whether you store your gear here with them, purchase it, or have it repaired, you are in remarkably good hands.

Phone: 01-987- 869-8116

(On 1a, between 85 & 90)

Beach Accessible Snorkeling

There is simply no question that to experience the true nature of these waters you most definitely need to go out to some of these world-famous reefs with an experienced guide. If by chance you are not into boats or the open water, there is still fairly decent shore access snorkeling available on the island. It may not resemble the experience you will receive viewing the reefs via boat and snorkel, but for novices and for those who are more easily impressed, the following options are available.

Keep in mind that even with all the recent protections that have been put into place for some of the shallow reefs (under 10 feet) close to shore, the sheer number of visitors in the past 30 years has caused serious damage to coral at most of these sites. You will still most definitely enjoy yourself exploring the crystal-clear waters at any of the following spots along the west coast of the island, especially at Chankanaab Park.

*Remember, ALL qualified snorkel guides must require the use of a surface vest for snorkeling.

Chankanaab Park $$

With crystal clear water, some excellent remaining examples of coral, and an infinite variety of fish, the waters off the beautiful beach at this island park still offer the best shore access snorkeling in all of Cozumel. The park has plenty of rental gear available for snorkeling, shaded palapas, lounge chairs, and even private cabanas for the ultimate park package. The entrance fee ranges widely depending on which package you choose, but it can range from $30.00-$270.00 depending on activities. While the park can be crowded, it is meticulously maintained and beautiful. Be sure to explore the paths through the jungle with its small lagoon and colorful fish, and the botanical gardens with hundreds of varieties of local flora.

There are buffet packages, zip lines, snorkel packages, and much more. Enjoy one of the island's greatest assets. Hours are 8:00 a.m.–4:00 p.m. daily.

(On the old road a mile or so south of the last cruise ship pier, Puerta Maya)

Playa Corona Beach Bar $$

Mentioned before in this book, the snorkeling just off Playa Corona is excellent and fairly quiet especially if you get there before 11:00 a.m. Bring your own gear or rentals are available.

(About a mile south of the entrance to Chankanaab Park)

Sky Reef $$

Just down the road from Playa Corona, Sky Reef has all the rental gear as well as very good snorkeling. These two are my favorites for a relaxing snorkel, or for a day typically far from large crowds.

(About a mile south of the entrance to Chankanaab Park)

The Money Bar $$

A tad larger than the above two locations, but once again, the shore access snorkeling here is still considered some of the best. You will see the Money Bar just before you reach Chankanaab.

Phone: 52-987-869-5140

(Maybe 2 miles south of the last cruise ship pier along the old road)

Playa Azul $$

Playa Azul is on the north end of town, it is quiet and beautiful, with a decent little beach and good snorkeling off the right portion of the beach especially.

Phone: 52-987-869-5175

(About 4 miles north of town, you will see the signs)

Punta Sur Park $$

Mentioned several times already in these pages, the snorkeling off the beach at the end of the park road is wonderful. The entrance fee of about $14.00, and either bring your own gear or snorkel gear is available for rent.

(The southern point of the island)

**There are other spots along the west coast old road (especially south of Sky Reef), and north of town past Buccanos with pretty good shore access snorkeling, but I hesitate to mention only because snorkeling should be done with others and with a vest. If you pass these areas, you will know. Practice safe and responsible snorkeling, and use a T-shirt or rash guard, leave the sun lotion in your bag.

WATERSPORTS

SURFING

YES, there is surfing on Cozumel, and there is no better individual on this island to introduce you to the sport, and to the east coast waves, than the ambassador and pioneer of Cozumel surfing, Nacho (Ignacio) Gutierrez. More than 3 decades ago while working at the old Sports Page Bar in town, he began working the waves on the islands rugged east side. Fast forward 30 years and Nacho now operates the largest surf school in the Yucatan from his humble headquarters out of El Pescador Restaurant on Cozumel's "other side." As he so well says himself, "if you don't stand up and surf, you don't pay."

As energetic and professional as they come, he has taught thousands and thousands the art of surfing. Locals and international visitors have been coming to Nacho for 20 plus years of instruction since he first opened his school, he is quite simply the best.

The waves here are not Hawaii, but for beginners and intermediates, it is an ideal spot to learn. Nacho himself has competed worldwide and has no deeper joy than to teach the sport to others with his remarkable patience. Ask him about his spearfishing, snorkel tours, and beach-side lunches to the islands remote northwest coast on his boat.

www.cozumelsurfing.com
Phone: 52-987-111-9290
(Playa Chen Rio and El Pescador Restaurant on the islands east side)

SAILING AND CATAMARAN TRIPS

Cozumel Sailing

Families, corporate groups, or any gathering will enjoy the stunning blue waters of Cozumel aboard the Tucan. Explore the northwest coast, maybe some trolling and deep-sea fishing, snorkeling if the conditions are right, and stop for a look at the deserted beaches up north in Cozumel. Sunset excursions or day-long trips are available. The maximum capacity is 28, but smaller groups are available.
Phone: 52-987-869-2312

Exclusive Cozumel Sailing

Luxury catamaran tours available anywhere from 4–6 hours which include snorkeling, kayaks, paddleboards, a delicious lunch, a full bar, sodas, bottled water and all aboard a new boat with AC cabins, and 4 bathrooms, for any size group up to 34 looking for a cruise in pampered relaxation and the beauty of the Caribbean.

Phone: 52-987-120-5601

Fury Catamarans

Probably not as intimate of an experience as Exclusive Cozumel Sailing, rather these excursions tend to be serious party boats, but if that's what you're into you'll find it here! For 20 years Fury has been operating 5 or so 65' custom catamarans with their combination sail, snorkel, and beach parties. All you can drink beer, sodas, and margaritas, with a complimentary lunch including burgers, and a buffet of salads and pastas. The tour also includes snorkel gear, fun, and a heated game of beach volleyball or hammocks, floats, and kayaks if you simply want to chill once you're on the beach.

Phone: 52-987-872-5145

ATLANTIS SUBMARINE

Yes, a submarine! See the depths and the reefs off Cozumel in a brilliantly visual, unique, and pampered fashion. The trip lasts around 2 hours and you will reach depths of up to 130' with a professional and fascinating narrative throughout. Children are welcome and will be wowed as will anyone, but kids must be a minimum of 3' tall. If this sounds at all intriguing you're not alone because space is always limited so it pays to reserve early. You will be tendered on a short 10-minute ride along the coast, where you will then be transferred to the submarine. Do not forget your camera for this trip. You will cruise through 30' coral heads amongst a universe of fish and spectacular color, slowly reaching a depth of 100'-130'. Adults $107.00 and kids $67.00, 5 trips daily.

Phone: 52-987-872-5671

FISHING CHARTERS

As with dive operators, it is always best to contact fishing services prior to arrival and to be sure of all the same safety measures you would look into before hiring a dive guide. The following have been around and have shown consistent excellence. Happy fishing!

Aquarius Fishing

For deep-sea or flat fishing, contact Aquarius and Captain Carlos Vega. The staff is bi-lingual, and each has 10–40 years of experience fishing and guiding in the waters off Cozumel, the Isla Blanca flats north of Cancun and up and down the Yucatan coast. Deep-sea for blue and white marlin, sailfish, and more, or test your fly-fishing skills in the flats off the northern coast of Cozumel for small tarpon, bonefish, barracuda, triggerfish, snook and permit depending on the season. Captain Vega was born and raised on the island and has been featured in magazines and publications such as Florida Sport Fishing, Cabella Outfitter, Salt Water Fly Fishing, and ESPN. The flat fishing in Cozumel's northern flats is an experience few have, or the Cancun office can arrange trips to the world-renowned Isla Blanca lagoon and flats north of Cancun. (1-800-371-2924)

Phone: 52-987-869-1096

Scuba Du

Since 1992, Scuba Du has been a highly recommended dive and snorkel outfit. With years of experience on the island, their expertise as a fishing charter service puts them over the top. Whether its deep-sea or flat fishing, Scuba Du will be happy to guide you to either location. Test your spin casting or fly-fishing technique in the sand flats off the northern coast of the island, or let them take you to the deep sea for a shot at marlin, dorado, and more.

Phone: 52-987-872-9505
(Located out of the El Presidente Hotel south of town)

Albatross Charters

Albatross provides some of Cozumel's finest deep-sea fishing. In season, fish for blue or white marlin, sailfish, snapper, grouper, dorado, and more. Kick back in their clean, comfortable, and well-maintained boats, top of the line gear, and learn the tricks from their bi-lingual guides. Albatross will combine half-day fishing with a half-day of diving in the reefs off the island. Island cruises, snorkel trips, and sunset cruises are all available from the masters at Albatross.

Phone: 987-872-7904
www.cozumel-fishing.com

Tres Hermanos

Since 2000 the great people and guides of Tres Hermanos have been leading guests on deep-sea and flat fishing trips. Also, they offer fishing and snorkeling options and scuba diving. They specialize in small groups of anglers for an amazing Cozumel experience.

Phone: 52-987-107-2030

PADDLE BOARDS/KITE BOARDING (SUPS OR STAND UP PADDLE BOARDS)

De Lille Sports $$$

One of Cozumel's greatest athletes, a 2-time world windsurf champion, 7-time Mexican champion, and a pioneer of kiteboarding and SUPs on the island, Raul De Lille is the owner of De Lille Sports. Raul brought kiteboarding to this island in 1999 and literally brought the first SUPs to the island as well.

The kiteboards are available for rent or purchase, as is instruction and certification. The SUPs available are some of his very own designs and Raul's passion for this sport is contagious. Schedule a night paddleboard outing with illuminated boards, or head up the remote northwest Cozumel coast and explore the sand flats and mangroves, or for the beginner, paddle up and down the Cozumel coast and just get your bearings. There are SUP experiences, but few like the options to those through Cozumel native Raul De Lille. Ask about their fishing and snorkel trips.

Phone: 52-1-987-103-6711
(The next door north of Hotel Barracuda, across from Mega just south of town)

LOCAL TRANSPORTATION

ULTRAMAR FERRY SCHEDULE BETWEEN COZUMEL AND PLAYA DEL CARMEN

As of 5/2020, the fare one way was 200 pesos, and round trip was 400 pesos for adults, which includes children over 12. There is a new first-class package for 260 pesos one way, and 500 pesos round trip, which gives you a wider reclining seat. Kids under 5 are free, and the child rate between 6–11 years of age is 160 pesos one way, or 320 pesos round trip. The trip is about 45 minutes each way.

Schedule from Playa Del Carmen-Cozumel:

7:00 a.m., 8:00 a.m., 10:00 a.m., noon, 2:00 p.m., 4:00 p.m., 6:00 p.m., 8:00 p.m., and 10:00 p.m.

Schedule from Cozumel-Playa Del Carmen:

5:45 a.m., 7:00 a.m., 9:00 a.m., 11:00 a.m., 1:00 p.m., 5:00 p.m., 7:00 p.m., 9:00 p.m.

Phone: 52-998-293-9092

www.ultramarferry.com

The ADO bus is the least expensive way to reach Playa Del Carmen from the Cancun airport and then ferry to Cozumel or vice versa. Prices and schedules can fluctuate so always check their website. Price is currently about $10.00 each way and the bus station in Playa del Carmen is an easy 3-minute walk to the ferry terminal. The bus station in Playa is located on the corner of 5th Avenue and Juarez. Each of the 4 Cancun airport terminals has bus service to and from Playa Del Carmen. Look for the big red ADO on the bus as you exit the terminal or ask, they will be very helpful. The buses all have AC, are VERY comfortable, and you will be assigned a seat with your ticket.

www.ado.com

BUS BETWEEN PLAYA DEL CARMEN AND CANCUN AIRPORT

The first bus from Playa Del Carmen to the airport leaves at 3:00 a.m., and then about every 40 minutes until 10:15 p.m. Always check the ADO website though as schedules can vary.

Bus Between Cancun Airport and Playa Del Carmen

The first bus from Cancun airport leaves at 12:45 a.m., then 1:30 a.m., 3:00 a.m., 8:00 a.m., and then every 40 minutes or so until midnight. Always check the ADO website though as schedules can vary.

PRIVATE TRANSFER SERVICES FROM CANCUN AIRPORT TO PLAYA DEL CARMEN

A bit more expensive, but completely hassle-free, are the several private transfer services shuttling travelers between Cancun airport and the ferry in Playa Del Carmen taking you to Cozumel, or any other destination in the Yucatan for that matter. I have used several and they are all excellent. They will pick you up in a comfortable van and quickly zip you to Playa. Most if not all are bi-lingual and extremely helpful and cordial. Depending on the number of passengers, each way from the airport to Playa Del Carmen averages $65.00-$80.00, and round-trip averages between $130.00-$160.00. The following are all excellent private transfer companies with stellar reputations.

www.usa-transfers.com

www.happyshuttlecancun.com

www.cancunandrivieramaya.com

FLY FROM CANCUN TO COZUMEL

For years, Mayair has been flying visitors from Cancun to Cozumel, a short 20-minute flight. Rates vary from $60.00 round trip to $100.00, depending on the season. It is always best to book and check rates directly through their website.
www.mayair.com

COZUMEL AIRPORT TO YOUR HOTEL OR SAN MIGUEL TOWN

You will essentially have four options once you reach the airport on how to get into town, or to your hotel. Cabs are NOT allowed onto the airport grounds, though a brief walk to the street out front of the airport where the roundabout is and the taxis will find you.

Rental Car

Whether you have one arranged ahead of time or not, there are several rental car kiosks once you leave customs.

Shared Shuttle

From the airport, you may have one of these arranged through your hotel prior to arrival, but if not, they will be out front as you clear customs. Depending on where you are going, a short jaunt to town, or the south end hotels or anything in between, rates will run from 100 to 250 pesos per person, possibly a bit more.

Private Shuttle

Same as above, rates for private shuttles should range between 220 pesos and 550 pesos, or more.

Taxis

As mentioned above, taxis can only be found off the airport grounds. It is a short 2-minute walk to the street out front of the airport, and if you are hungry, look for the red tent across the street and stop in at Diegos Tacos for excellent tacos and cold lemonade. Rates to the ferry pier in town should be around 100 pesos, north end hotels between 250 and 500 pesos, and south end hotels could range anywhere from 300 pesos to 800 pesos. Always ask prior to getting in a cab.

BICYCLE RENTALS

Cycling the island is easy and fun, whether you choose to bomb around town, head to the north end on the quiet and only street, or circumnavigate the island, the following are excellent rental options. Helmets are required and will be included in your rental as will a lock.

www.rentabikecozumel.com There is no brick and mortar shop on the island, but your options are clear via their website. Your cycle can be delivered to you anywhere on the island. These bikes are well-maintained, and the selection is excellent. Cost ranges between $25.00-$60.00 per day depending on the bike.

www.bestbikescozumel.com On ave. 10, just north of Juarez are some decent bikes and snorkel gear for rent. Best Bikes has one-speed cruisers, and multi-geared great quality bikes ranging from $10.00 per day to $20.00 per day. Check out the website for photos and rates, the bikes here are excellent unless you are looking for something of a touring variety and much higher quality.

Phone: 52-987-878-8602

www.beachbumbikescozumel.com Electric bicycle tours are available here for groups, or rental of electric bikes, even a tandem is an option. Nonelectric bikes are available here as well for around $25.00 per day. E-bikes rent for $35.00/6 hours and the tandem is $45.00/6 hours. About 3–4 miles south of town on the main ocean road, directly next door to Eagle Rider Harley Davidson.

Phone: 52-987-688-5003

CAR AND SCOOTER RENTALS

There are many on the island, or that you will find online, and I cannot speak for any of them. What I can do is speak for the outstanding service I and thousands of others have had with Margarita and her staff at Isis Rental for many, many years. ***(www.isiscarrental.com)*** Her shop is located a brief walk from the town square **on 5, between 2 & 4**. They will very carefully go over each vehicle with you, making note of any dings or dents, there are no surprises at Isis rental. Insurance will be included in all rentals. Please take the time to read the following about vehicle rentals on the island, AND you will see I highly discourage scooter rentals for anyone.

Tourists and locals alike use cars and scooters all over the island, but please accept these words of caution. Always wear your helmet if renting a moped, it is required by law, and you will be ticketed if not wearing one. When touring the island, you will likely be stopping at many bars and restaurants. If on a moped I can't stress enough the devastating consequences you will face either physically or financially if you either cause an accident or are injured in one. Moped accidents happen daily either due to drinking or inexperience, but whatever the reason is, you will regret your mistake for the rest of your life. If you insist on riding a scooter, never drive after dark, please do not drive drunk, and watch for gravel, potholes, or animals in the road, and most importantly obey all road signs and watch for other drivers. The best suggestion for touring the island is to hire a cab ($100.00/4 hours to tour the island), rent a car, and if possible, always have a designated driver. I don't mean to preach or to be a bummer, it is reality.

Do not be fooled by thinking your automobile insurance back home will cover expenses here if you have an accident. More often than not you WILL be detained on the island until all expenses are covered. Your domestic insurance carrier is not recognized in Mexico. Whenever renting a vehicle, always be extremely thorough in your vehicle inspection. Taking pictures may seem extreme, but it is always a good idea, as well as checking underneath the vehicle for any damage there before leaving. In short, check your vehicle from top to bottom for any dents and scratches, and be sure to verify all problems with your rental car personnel. Pictures are the best proof you have if a problem occurs. Keep in mind, for vehicle rentals you will need a valid driver's license, a major credit card, and you typically need to be 21. Have fun and drive carefully.

Phone: 52-984-879-3111

Cozumel's Green Angels is a service for stranded motorists. They regularly patrol the island, and typically for free, will assist you or tow you, if you find yourself broken down on the road. They are NOT someone to call if you simply need repair, rather the Green Angels are there when most needed for stranded motorists.
Phone: 52-987-871-0296

TAXIS

You will see taxis everywhere on the island except for the more remote east side, though when hired they will of course go there. Nearly anywhere along the west coast from town to either of the 3 cruise ship piers or beyond at the south beach clubs, you will see or be able to flag down a cab. Be sure to confirm a price before you get in, but the drivers are generally pretty cool and straightforward. Prices in town to other locations in town should be under 150 pesos. If you choose to have a cab take you from town to the south end beach clubs, or the north end of the island, or the east side, prices will range between $8.00-$30.00 to south end beach clubs depending on distance, and $60.00 to the east side of the island. ***www.cozumeltaxitours.com*** is an excellent local family run private taxi service with lots of options if families, groups, or individuals are looking for a tour of the island.

MISCELLANEOUS SERVICES AND INFORMATION

A BRIEF HISTORY OF THE AREA: (THE GRINGO TRAIL, SIESTAS AND WHEN EVERYTHING WAS LOCAL)

The Gringo Trail is a long-time moniker by which travelers have designated destinations from Mexico to Guatemala to Peru and beyond in their quest for remote travel, ruins, beaches, villages, and spiritual revelation. While the term is still used today by some, it was as recent as 30–40 years ago that backpackers from around the world sought Cozumel, Isla Mujeres, the remote beaches and small town of Playa del Carmen, the stunning ruins of Uxmal, Chichen-Itza, and Tulum, or Xcalak and Mahajual, referred to then as Mexico's coconut coast, or the sanctity of Oaxaca. They were still travel destinations that took work to reach. Either overland through Mexico, or by air to

Chetumal or Merida, and bus or hitchhiking from there-these were your options until and after Cancun's airport opened in 1974 and slowly began to change everything. I traveled via Chetumal and sometimes Merida for the most part until 1980.

Cozumel's place on the trail was in part due to that until the early-mid '70s, literally no infrastructure existed along the coast aside from Isla Mujeres, Tulum, and Cozumel. Cozumel was a welcome oasis of sorts as it was the only bed, restaurant or cold beer between Merida and Chetumal, aside from Isla Mujeres, there was little else aside from beaches to pitch a tent. But mostly, as today, Cozumel was a community that embraced those of us visiting in the earlier days with open arms and a graciousness that is still evident in the people of the island today.

Playa Del Carmen was an adventure either accomplished with a VW bug you may have rented in Merida, hitchhiking, an occasional bus, or by asking for a ride on one of the few "ice trucks" delivering chunks of ice to fishing villages along the coast. My first introduction to Playa Del Carmen was being dropped off at the tiny crooked white sign saying Playa Del Carmen and walking east along the sand street toward the smell of saltwater. It was the clatter of a few barking dogs, some run-down homes or huts with palm frond roofs, a handful of old rusty cars along the way, and after a 30–40-minute walk, the small village appeared with an ocean as crystal clear and blue, unlike anything I had ever seen.

Cozumel was the goal and the ferry would come once in the morning to carry whatever handful of travelers, but mostly locals working on the island, and supplies from the mainland. There wasn't really a schedule, but it would arrive in the morning for passengers and then return once in the evening bringing mainland workers back to their homes. The ferry was more to supply and transport a mainland workforce for Cozumel and its fledgling tourist industry, its few hotels, restaurants, and bars.

This of course would all change as Cozumel's tourist industry exploded and then with the construction of Playa's Hotel Molcas as the town's first hotel and its grandiose veranda lined with dining tables draped in white linens. Playa Del Carmen was born and would never look back. Its pockets of stunning white beach as recently as the late '70s hemmed in with outcropping stone were forever changed as the developers dynamited the outcropping stone that held the sand in place for many millennia to achieve even more beach. They have been fighting to keep the sand in place ever since, especially south of the ferry pier in what is today referred to as Playacar.

Tulum's place on the Gringo Trail was equally as significant. It was the stunning Maya ruins (the only significant Maya fortification on the coast), and those responsible for the early days of cenote exploration and wreck diving that introduced Tulum to the world. My first taste of Tulum was in '78, and there were six little rooms along the coast owned by a young Italian where we stayed, and our only water was from the bucket well in the small Maya town nearby. The beaches, few visitors and ruins made for a uniquely mystical place.

Today's Hwy. 307 between Cancun and Tulum was a narrow-paved road with the ever-encroaching jungle always trying to take it back. It was difficult to not be struck by foliage as your vehicle passed through. Akumal and its stunning shore access shallow coral reef was the home to the mainland's first-ever "resort," Club Akumal Caribe, still in operation today. That shallow reef is gone today, but the turtles remain and return each year to Akumal's beaches for nesting. Don Pablo Bush Romero and a handful of divers and investors started this small resort. In 1974, I had the pleasure of visiting Akumal and this small pioneering resort with my parents via a rented VW bug and a long ride from Merida. Our friends from Milwaukee were among the initial investors and dear friends of Bush Romero, recognized as the "founder" of Akumal, and a forerunner of wreck diving and cenote exploration in the Yucatan peninsula.

Even as the coast from Puerto Juarez to Tulum continues to be embedded in concrete and resorts, it is unknown to most visitors that much of the coast remains natural and has been preserved in perpetuity with the establishment of significant Biosphere Reserves. Most notable are Sian Ka'an just south of Tulum and Rio Celestun Biosphere Reserve on the Yucatan's north coast. Many villages and communities remain along the coast that are reminiscent of the Yucatan's early days. It is the beauty of this part of Mexico, and all you need to do is explore. The maze of resorts known as the Riviera Maya is only about 75 miles long and for now, aside from that, much of the Yucatan peninsula remains as it was years ago.

As of 2016, the creation of The Mexican Caribbean Biosphere Reserve has implemented more significant regulations to be enforced by the Mexican Navy and SEMARNAT (The Secretary of Environment and Natural History of Mexico) in perpetuity prohibiting oil exploration within the Mesoamerican Reef and designed to further protect the coastlines fragile ecosystem.

This is a tall order, but its implementation is a solid step in working to understand and minimize the effects development has had on the intricately complex ecosystem of vital filtrating coastal mangroves, beach, lagoons, bird-life, fisheries, sewage and protecting the freshwater cenotes and their utmost importance, as the only source of fresh water on the mainland, and one of the world's largest underground cave systems.

Unless one travels inland to smaller villages of the Yucatan, the **"Siesta"** is something rarely experienced by travelers these days, unless they are sleeping off cocktails. Really though, as recently as 30 years ago in Playa Del Carmen, Cozumel, Isla Mujeres, or any of these seaside towns and islands, the towns completely shut down and stores closed from early afternoon until 5.00 p.m. or so, and residents relaxed in the heat of the day. Prior to tourism when local economies were fully reliant on fishing and agriculture, there was no reason to stay open mid-afternoon. More and more outside visitors have virtually eliminated the siesta from many communities who rely on tourism, but it is still common in Mexico, Latin America, and Mediterranean countries in the heat of the day as the custom has for centuries. If you travel to small villages not reliant on tourism, even 5–10 miles inland in the Yucatan, in some ways, life is somewhat as it was 200 or more years ago, including the siesta.

Not to dwell on the past, but its perspective is important in understanding how quickly, dramatically, and life-changing to many the development along the Caribbean coastline of Mexico has been. If you think of the '70's when this coast was a virtual jungle, nearly untouched by human hands, it is amazing what has transpired. Today, travel guides and travelers are in search of what is **"local,"** from quiet beaches to the few operating restaurant remnants from the early days, "when everything was local." In the not too distant past, there were very few places with tacos, tamales, lobster, beans, fresh seafood, a cold beer, and yes, sea turtle was on virtually all menus. The development has, of course, included a supply chain to support it, and that includes the ability of restaurants, resorts, shops, and bars to quench the many international tastes of those from all over the world who desire more than what just the local population once provided those who came here years ago. It is quite simply an example of tourism and how quickly it can take hold and change any place on earth.

ISLAND CHARITIES

FB@ Cozumel Chrysalis Group (Provides financial and supply support to island students in need)

FB@ Cruz Roja Cozumel (Cozumel Red Cross)

FB@ Humane Society of Cozumel Island

FB@ DIF Cozumel (Supports needy families of Cozumel)

FB@ Agrupacion Musical Communitaria Banda Sinfonica de Cozumel (The local youth symphony and needed supplies)

FB@ Cozumel Ocean Research

FB@ Cozumel Coral Reef Restoration

FB@ Friends of Cozumel (Benefiting island individuals and families in need)

FB@ Ciudad de Angeles (A Christian children's home.)

FB@ Otono Cultural Cozumel (Supporting the arts with a 5-day free fall festival open to all. Dance, art classes, indigenous dance, local and international music, symphony, ballet, seminars and more.)

www.caritasquintanaroo.org Food bank for needy families in the Yucatan, Isla Mujeres, and Cozumel

COZUMEL, A GROWING DESTINATION FOR CYCLISTS

Cozumel will host its 12th annual International Triathlon this year (2020) on November 22nd. Twenty-one riders of this competition will qualify for the World Championships in Hawaii. So, what came first here, the bike or the triathlon? Well the bike of course, but the interest in cycling has soared since these races have come to the island. Not only with expat and international riders here to train, but smaller races are being held on Cozumel, and locals are out riding in numbers never before seen. They are not just riding, but they are buying good road bikes, all the gear, it is an amazing thing to see here. Bicycle lanes are painted and evident downtown as you would have never seen even 6 years ago. Still though, regardless of bike lanes, local drivers do not necessarily recognize these lanes, so always cycle with caution and never assume if you are in a bike lane that all is good.

Aside from this, circumnavigating the island has become more and more cycle-friendly, with more of the route dedicated to only cyclists, with clearly marked roads and large lanes.

1. North from the airport road is a 10-mile round trip ride going north to Cozumel Country Club and back. This is not cycle exclusive, but the road is wide and fairly quiet. The road north from the Cozumel Country Club is slowly being paved another 5 miles or so, north to the Isla Passion dock.
2. Navigate your way south from town about 5 miles along the oceanfront road, pass the last cruise ship pier (Puerta Maya), and the road will split. Follow signs toward Chankanaab Park to your right and you will be on the old west coast road. The cycling here offers a quiet stretch south for some 20 miles until you reach Palancar

Beach Club. Once you reach Palancar, cars are forced to merge onto the new road, and cyclists have the old road to themselves for another 4–5 miles of beautiful riding until you reach Punta Sur Park on the island's southern point.

3. From Punta Sur, riders will head north and almost immediately you will see some rocks blocking the old road and signs asking vehicles to merge onto the new road. This stretch is cycle only as well and will take you on a cycle road nearly all the way north (except for a mile or two where the roads merge) to Mezcalito's, a stretch of nearly 15 miles. The two roads are parallel and run along the remarkably scenic east coast road for some of the best riding on the island.

4. Once you reach Mezcalito's Bar, the road turns west and heads back to town for about an 11-mile ride. There is a bike lane nearly the entire way to town. Be careful though as scooters and slow cars sometimes use this lane as well, but for the most part, it is smooth sailing for the cyclist until you reach town.

In short, the days for cyclists on Cozumel have come a long way and it is recognized as the Yucatan's premier cycling destination with amazing views, good roads, and flat terrain ideal for the beginner, the intermediate, advanced or cyclist in training. *(www.ironman.com/im-cozumel)*

CERVECERIA PUNTA SUR

The islands first, and currently only brewpub. A fun destination for the beer lover and pizza fanatic. The wood-fired pizzas are as good as the beer! Since 2017.

www.cerveceriapuntasur.com
(On 10, between A. R. Salas and 3)

KUN CHE PARK

Open Monday – Saturday from 10:00 a.m.–3:00 p.m. in the old town of El Cedral south of San Miguel town by about 15 miles. A park dedicated to visually involving guests into the ancient Mayan culture and to experience that life. "Discover the Mayan Lifestyle," they say. Watch as the ancient ballgame Pok T Pok is played in front of your eyes, see tortilla making, and many more ancient Mayan traditions as if you were a part of that world. Check their website for much more information.

https://kunchepark.com/ - $25.00-$80.00 depending on the option you choose.
Phone: 52-1-987-111-5611

PUEBLO DEL MAIZ

A surprisingly fun experience where you just might not expect it! An entertaining one-hour tour into the ancient Mayan world with interactive music, dance and an immersion into the art, and history, of tortilla making, grinding cacao into chocolate, the Mayan world of honey making, and all in a fun theatrical way. Sort of like a live museum in a replicated ancient Mayan village. Kids of any age will enjoy this experience, as will adults. Admission is about $25.00 for adults.

(On the transversal road about 5 miles east of town on the south side of the road, you will see the signs) (FB@pueblodelmaiz) Open 9:00 a.m.–4:00 p.m. daily.

GOOD CLINICS, DOCTORS, AND HOSPITALS

The medical care available on the island is outstanding. More often than not though, while care is far more affordable on the island than in the states, typically you will pay cash as your insurance is rarely recognized here. Options abound though. If seeking medical attention in Cozumel, they may require proof of insurance and a copy of a major credit card. Prior to travel ask your insurance carrier all the details to clearly understand the limits of your coverage during your trip. Some may have an arrangement for reimbursement of expenses when you return home. (Costamed clinic in Cozumel has such arrangements, as does The Cozumel International Hospital). If you are not comfortable with the policies of your domestic health insurance carrier back home, the following Health Travel Insurance organizations have excellent track records for coverage when traveling to Mexico.

*DAN Travel Insurance
www.diversalertnetwork.org and www.worldnomads.com

San Miguel Clinic
www.hospitalmsm.com
Phone: 52-987-872-0103
(In town on 6 between 5 & 10)

Amerimed
www.amerimedcozumel.com
Phone: 52-987-869-5555
(A.R. Salas, between 85 & 85 bis)

Costamed
www.costamed.com.mx
Phone: 52-987-872-9400
(On 1 between 50 & 55)

*I was referred and came here for an incident late one night on my bicycle when I was hit in the head by a large fruit bat! The doctor greeted me pleasantly in perfect English and examined my head for any injury. He looked at me with a smile and said, "That bat was probably more scared than you were, you'll be fine." I was charged nothing for a 20-minute visit. I will always recommend Costamed.

The Cozumel International Hospital
www.hospitalcozumel.com
Phone: 52-987-872-1430, or for emergencies 52-987-116-7531
(In town on 5, between Rafael Melgar and 5)

Dr. Bonnie Piccolo at the San Miguel Clinic
Phone: 52-987-872-3070

Dr. Juan Jose Arellano
House or hotel room calls with a reputation of excellence on the island. (24/7 Medical Service and House Calls Cozumel)
Phone: 52-987-104-1713, FB@urg24

EXCELLENT LOCAL HOTELS/GUEST HOUSES

Hotel Mary Carmen
This centrally located, very clean, and affordable island hotel has been a favorite of mine and thousands of others for many years. No pool, but a nice breakfast each morning and comfortable common areas for guests. Enjoy the resident turtles in the downstairs common area.
www.hotelmarycarmen.com.mx
(Just south of the town square on the pedestrian walk)

Hotel Flamingo

Just a brief 5-minute walk from the square and the Playa Del Carmen ferry pier is this long-time island favorite. Great cocktails at the hotel bar with quiet live music most weekends. There are 18 beautifully appointed rooms and suites at affordable prices.

https://www.hotelflamingo.com
Phone: 52-987-872-1264
(On 6, between Rafael Melgar and 50)

Blue Angel Dive Resort

Funky and beautiful, and located directly on the water, though on the busy oceanfront road just under 2 miles south of town. The 20 some odd rooms and outdoor grassy common area for guests are just gorgeous. The views and sunsets are always a treat here. Dine at the hotel restaurant which is excellent, or explore some of the dining options nearby. Dive and snorkel packages are available at this long time Cozumel institution directly from their pier and boats out front.

www.blueangelresort.com

Hotel Caribe

For decades this small and unassuming little hotel has held its own on the island. I stayed here 40 years ago, and as recently as 2019! With a small pool, an outdoor common area with tables and chairs, hot coffee each morning, and a staff that is always helpful. Hotel Caribe is a great choice for the budget traveler or simply those looking for a quiet little spot 5 minutes from town that won't break the budget.

On 2, between 15 & 20.

Hotel Bello Caribe

The jungle foliage in the hotel lobby is inviting enough here at Hotel Bello Caribe. Another of my favorite little local hotels, though it is a good 15-minute walk from town. There is a pool in the back that is rarely used, but always clean and chilly! All rooms have AC, they are tidy and very comfortable. I love the second-floor common area looking down on the beautiful hacienda like lobby. The Sunday buffet here is excellent, always packed, about $10.00, and has to be one of the best buffets on the island at that price!

(On Ave. 30, between 12 & 14)

Baldwins Guest House

If quiet, cozy, and peaceful are what you are in search of, Baldwins is an ideal choice for pampered comfort and quiet. A 20-minute walk from town, and a block from Casa Mission, one of Cozumel's best restaurants. There are four lovely rooms and a private cabana for families or groups. Baldwins consistently boasts 5-star ratings. The guest house features a large pool surrounded by lush gardens with over 400 varieties of plants. There are hammocks and loungers throughout, and a screened gazebo for gatherings day or night. Breakfast and a nightly happy hour are included, and in addition there is a nice outdoor kitchen for guests to use. This place is simply beautiful.

www.baldwinsguesthousecozumel.com
USA/Canada Phone: 770-934-6987, or locally 52-987-872-1148
(Ave. 55, between 1 and A. R. Salas)

Hacienda San Miguel Hotel and Suites

Seemingly far away from the hustle of downtown, yet only a 10-minute walk, the quiet ambiance of this gorgeous property is hard to beat on the island. Beautiful gardens with 11 impeccably appointed studio rooms and suites.

www.haciendasanmiguel.com
USA: 1-866-712-6387, or locally 52-987-872-1986
(On 10, between Rafael Melgar and 5)

Villablanca Dive Hotel

Another long-standing dive hotel on the oceanside road south of town, but set back off the busy street. Villablanca is ideal for families, groups, or individuals, whether you are divers or not. The lawns and gardens are beautiful so relax around the pool with other guests discussing the day's events, or make the pool your event! With 50 rooms, 3 villas and a private penthouse, a tennis court for guests, jacuzzi, an on-call doctor, laundry service, babysitting service, car, bicycle rentals, and much more. Villablanca is simple and exquisite. Dive shops are on-site with all you need, and their two docks and selection of dive boats leave from directly across the street.

www.villablanca.net
Phone: 52-987-872-0730
(On the main oceanside road about 2 miles south of town)

Hotel Ventanas Al Mar

Located on the islands only cliff, far away from any congestion or noise, along the rugged and beautiful east coast of Cozumel. Actually, Ventanas Al Mar is the ONLY hotel on this side of the island, and as they say, "A million-star hotel," offering a hint at the universe of stars you will see nightly from your room and balcony overlooking the Caribbean, it is breathtaking! With a small pool and outdoor lobby, this hotel provides the ultimate in peace and relaxation on the island. It is ideal for a honeymoon or romantic getaway.

www.ventanasalmarcozumel.com

SOME ALL-INCLUSIVE RESORT OPTIONS

- **Playa Azul Golf Scuba Spa Hotel (www.playa-azul.com)**
- **Hotel Cozumel and Resort (www.hotelcozumel.com.mx)**
- **Presidente Inter-Continental Resort and Spa (www.presidenteicozumel.com)**
- **Sunscape Sabor Cozumel (www.sunscaperesorts.com)**
- **Secrets Aura Cozumel (www.secretsresorts.com)**
- **Coral Princess Golf and Dive Resort (www.coralprincess.com)**

ISLA PASSION

A stunningly beautiful sliver of land off Cozumel's northwest coast where desolation awaits you, as does a small part of this island (actually it isn't exactly an island, rather it is a speck of land connected to the mainland) reserved as an All-Inclusive destination for day trips. Several small tour operators will stop here, avoiding the northwest corner of Isla Passion reserved for the party crowd. The bone-fishing is remarkable in the nearby sand flats. If you travel north toward the Cozumel Country Club, the road sort of ends,

BUT work is being done to pave the remaining 5 miles or so which takes you to a pier and boat launches where for a couple of hundred pesos, you can hire a small skiff to take you out to the island. Once you reach the end of the road here, you can see Isla Passion, it is only a 5-minute boat ride or a great place to bring a kayak!

PUNTA MOLAS (COZUMEL'S REMOTE NORTHWEST POINT)

Difficult to reach, but quite simply the most remote and magnificent point in all of Cozumel. There is a very rough sand road which heads north on the east coast of the island from Mezcalito's Restaurant, though you will not make it in a jeep or rental car so DO NOT even attempt it. You will get stuck and your insurance will be void! There are two very special options though to reach the lighthouse there, and the most remote part of the island. This is not for everyone, as both trips are tough and time-consuming, but you will be in experienced hands on both tours.

ADRIAN OF COZUMEL

An adventure by boat with one of the island's best guides renowned for his years of experience on the island. Adrian knows this part of Cozumel better than most, and the tour includes lunch, snorkeling over wrecks and remote reefs, trekking through knee-deep water to the coast, and climbing the lighthouse for amazing views. See a part of the island few do, with a fascinating, fun, and informative guide who will show you many secrets of the Cozumel jungles, lagoons, and hidden ruins of the ancient Maya. Cost app. $350.00 for 1–2 guests, $90.00 additional per guest with a maximum of 6. Check out Adrian's website for more cool options offered by this Cozumel native.

www.adriancozumel.com

THE LIGHTHOUSE PROJECT

An overland adventure via custom dune buggies will take you along the rugged east coast to the Punta Molas lighthouse. On the way, you will see a cenote deep in the jungles, small Mayan ruins, and a coastline unseen by 99.99% of Cozumel visitors. The photo options and thrilling experience with this extremely conscientious tour will be something very special. Please take the time to read more about the Lighthouse Project and this tour on their website.

www.offroadcozumeltours.com

THE COZUMEL PEARL FARM

Truly one of Cozumel's most fascinating and unique experiences! Located on a remote stretch of gorgeous beach away from everything and in an island protected area, a trip here is like nothing else you will experience anywhere, not just on Cozumel. Originating in 2001 and opened to the public in 2012, this is the only pearl farm in the entire Caribbean. Daily tours involve a maximum of 8 guests and

include a tour and an education about this incredible project, snorkeling pure shallow reefs with a visual of how the pearls are created, and how the oysters are raised. Plenty of time will be left to relax on the beach with a magnificent shore lunch, to have a swim, snorkel, or just stroll the beach where you will be alone except for the other guests. The day tour via boat is from 10:00 a.m.–4:00 p.m. Adults $110.00, kids 6–12 are $85.00, and under 5 are free.

An ultimate aside are the overnight experiences this local family provides on their pristine beach and lagoon setting. Cabins are on the way and currently, tents are provided, but evenings are by the fire, under the stars, and Cozumel's endlessly dark sky far from any lights! A marvelous meal will be cooked for you, and the evening is yours in the island's most romantic, natural, and beautiful location. If there were a tour, or an evening to be spent, where you would remember and talk about for a lifetime, it would be a night at Cozumel's Pearl Farm. Adults $225.00, kids 6–12 are $175.00, and under 5 are free.

https://www.cozumelpearlfarm.mx/

COZUMEL BAR HOP

The original and best east side tour of the island, where if a party, safe drinking, and loads of fun are your goal, the Cozumel Bar Hop is your answer. The east coast of the island as you have already read in these pages is remote, there is no electricity, but the beauty is remarkable. You will stop at 4 small beach bars where your fee ($57.00 per person) gets you professional and informative transportation in comfortable small buses, a shot at each bar, and a T-shirt. Bring cash with you as there are no credit cards accepted over here, and any food and drink aside from that included is on you. The trip lasts about 5 hours. Great for corporate outings or groups of friends, bachelor or bachelorette parties, or any gathering. You will stop at Punta Morena, Coconuts, El Pescador, and Rastas beach bars for maybe 45 minutes at each separate place. Find out more on their website and have a blast! There is a minimum of 6 people per excursion, but nearly any size group can be accommodated.

www.cozumelbarhop.com

CHANKANAAB PARK

A Cozumel ecological treasure that is somewhat Disney-like, yet remarkably beautiful. While crowded at times, there is ample room in the expansive property for you to not be crammed in and to feel relaxed with the incredible options available for visitors. Zip-lines, snorkeling, sunning, lovely beaches, and all kinds of other activities, some of which need not be mentioned, in this very cool island park. Entrance fees are across the board depending on which activities you choose to partake in, so it is best to go to their website. Enjoy Chankanaab!

https://www.cozumelparks.com/en/

CELEBRATIONS AND IMPORTANT LOCAL HOLIDAYS

One of the island's largest festivals is **Carnival,** celebrated with parades, costumes, dancing, music, and fireworks, all in honor of the Caribbean heritage. Typically, **Carnival** falls on the 5 days before Ash Wednesday in February.

The International Bill Fishing Tournament typically held in May brings fishermen to the island from all over the world in search of the record marlin and sailfish.

The Santa Cruz Fiesta held in the tiny town of El Cedral each year on the first weekend of May. Honoring the town's patron saint, and El Cedral's place in Cozumel history with parades, rodeos, parties, and a large market

Cinco De Mayo is NOT Mexican Independence Day, rather it is a relatively insignificant holiday in Mexico where the difficult Mexican victory over the French in the Battle of Puebla is recognized. Still, lots of gringos and expats will celebrate the May 5th tradition in local restaurants and bars.

Mexican Independence Day is September 16th and is celebrated in town with stages, music, late-night dancing, parties, and fireworks. One of the most recognized times of the year locally, it is a big party!

San Miguel Archangel Festival each year on September 28th commemorates fallen fishermen when boaters carry a statue of Cozumel's patron saint by decorated boats, to the islands north end and toss flowers and garlands into the sea to honor those lost.

Dia De Muertos (Day of the Dead) is a celebration honoring the dead with parades and visits to graveyards supporting the spiritual journey of those who passed away. Begins October 31st-November 2nd each year. A colorful, eerie, and beautiful annual festival honoring family.

Virgin of Guadalupe Festival begins December 12th in earnest with church services and parades beginning what is referred to as Navidad Posadas, or Las Posadas, a 12-day celebration of the Christmas season. Friends and family gathering for evening meals, parties, and thanks, all culminating Christmas Eve with a midnight feast. Virgin Guadalupe is Mexico's patron saint and this one of the country's most important festivals and seasons.

WANT TO RENT OR BUY, GOOD LOCAL REALTORS

Both these women are highly respected and will work diligently to help find your dream property on this island.

Karen Bloemhoff (https://karencozumelrealestate.com/)

Patsy Chilson (www.patsychilsonrealtor.com)

SAFETY, ETIQUETTE, AND BEHAVIOR

Cozumel has kept itself relatively crime-free, but like anywhere discretion is your best policy. Do not flaunt anything of significant value, and late at night if you find yourself walking along dark beaches or streets, it is always a good idea to be with a friend. I have never experienced a problem here in nearly 45 years, but be smart and always be aware. Always lock your room or rental home, this is just common sense. Do not let the sense of vacation or friendly nature of the island allow you to drop your guard, enjoy and be smart.

Regarding etiquette, this should be common sense as well, but I am never surprised by the behavior of some. Loud and boisterous, or vulgar language will get you nowhere here. Tropical or not, unless you are at the beach, wear a shirt around town if you are a male, and even if you are gorgeous, save the bikini for the beach. Cozumel is a community, there are children and families, some of great faith, and while there is acceptance of minimal beachwear, you look obnoxious when shirtless, or wearing a bikini or speedo in town.

Be polite when dining, drinking, or shopping-locals have little tolerance for insolence and will treat you with little interest respectively. Respect goes a long way to enjoying your vacation and with those you meet on the island. I hear frustration often from diners that they must wait and wait for their bill at the end of a meal. In Mexico, it is considered impolite for the server to bring the bill in a restaurant until it is requested. All you need to do is ask and you will receive your bill. (La cuenta por favor, or the bill please).

You are in a foreign country and remember that consequences for bad decisions or behavior can result in unfortunate circumstances that may be very different than at home. Police are quite tolerant, but drinking and driving is not one where you will find any tolerance. Be safe, be humble, have fun, and enjoy.

EXCHANGING MONEY (FOREIGN CURRENCY/ DOLLARS VS. PESOS)

The most frequent question I get is should I use dollars or pesos? Pesos are of course the local currency, though you can easily use US dollars, Euros, or pesos. BUT any vendor has the right to impose their own exchange rate and therefore the rate of exchange to you. Rates are typically posted. In other words, if the official exchange rate is let's say, 20 to 1, a restaurant has the right to accept your US dollars at a rate of 12 to 1 which means you will be coming up well short when receiving your change. The bottom line is that pesos are best, and they will stretch your dollar further. Whether you are visiting for the day from the mainland or are here for however long, it is best to either bring pesos with you, exchange at a local ATM upon arrival, or at the airport, or one of the following locations on the island. If exchanging at an ATM, try to use one in a bank or supermarket, and not at an outside ATM where skimming machines can more easily be installed to steal your card information.

It is important to not leave your ATM card in the machine anywhere! It is amazing how often people leave their cards behind. Keep your wits about you when using these machines, your card could be quite difficult to recover if you leave it behind. Finally, you are typically required to show your passport when exchanging money at a bank. Banks open at 9:00 a.m. and close usually by 5:00 p.m. and are closed Sundays. Banco Azteca in the Elektra stores is an exception to this rule. They are open 8:00 a.m.- 9:00 p.m. daily with a restriction of $300.00 exchanged daily and are my favorite on the island when exchanging cash.

There are several banks around the town square (Parque Benito Juarez) in the center of town adjacent to the Playa Del Carmen ferry pier where you can exchange foreign currency, or with inside ATM's safe for use.

The Elektra appliance stores house **Banco Azteca** inside their stores, and they are excellent locations with long hours for exchange. They have a maximum of $300.00 daily and a passport is required. 8:00 a.m.-9:00 p.m. daily.

Elektra/Banco Azteca Locations Look for the bright yellow storefront!
(Avenue Juarez between 15 & 20, and calle 11, one block east of the oceanside road)

The Mega Supermarket Is a popular spot for locals with several ATM's. A short walk from downtown.
(Just south of calle 11, and on the oceanside road)

PHARMACIES

You will see pharmacies everywhere, and while most are fine, there are a couple we will note here that are well-respected and trusted on the island. All of these have a doctor on staff.

Farmacia Del Ahorro
(Ave. Juarez, between 25 & 30)

Farmacia Dori
(A.R. Salas, between 20 & 25)

The Mega Supermarket has an excellent pharmacy inside.

SEAFOOD (OUT OF SEASON DATES)

Many people may be unaware that some of the most popular seafood items available in local restaurants have specific seasons where their harvest is strictly illegal. Read the following and opt to simply not order the item if you see it on a menu when you know it is "out-of-season." They may say it is frozen and it may very well be, or not. Simply not ordering is the best option. Unfortunately, the enforcement of these off-season regulations can be lax at best. The following dates are "out-of-season or en veda," and it is illegal to harvest certain species of seafood.

Conch (May 1ˢᵗ-October 31ˢᵗ)

Octopus (December 16ᵗʰ-July 31ˢᵗ)

Lobster (March 31ˢᵗ-June 30ᵗʰ)

Grouper (February 15ᵗʰ-March 15ᵗʰ)

****These seasons may vary slightly by year.**

"Try not to be a man of success, but rather try to become a man of value".

Albert Einstein

WEATHER SUMMARY

The rainy season runs from late May usually into October, nearly the same as the hurricane season. With the ocean breezes, it is still quite nice along the water in late spring and summer, and rain is most common in the afternoon. The stormiest months are usually in the fall, toward the end of the rainy season. Nortes are common December through February, creating some of the coolest temperatures of the season, bringing strong winds at times from the north, often closing the ports for dive and fishing boats.

Temperature Range by Month (Fahrenheit)

January: 60–80

February: 65–90

March: 70–90

April: 75–95

May: 80–100

June: 75–100

July: 75–100

August: 75–100

September: 70–90

October: 70–95

November: 70–90

December: 65–80

PACKING SUGGESTIONS/TRAVEL TIPS

I am as light a packer as there is, but below is a culmination of 40+ years of packing suggestions for this part of the world.

- Casual shorts, T-shirts, sundresses, sandals, and for sure walking shoes if you plan on walking any distance. Women will want a beach wrap, or two – buy one when you visit, they can be worn for nearly any occasion. It is a good idea to bring along a light jacket, sweatshirt or a light sweater. Some nights can be breezy and cool, or if you get sunburned, you may want something comfy in the evening for the chill.
- A photocopy of the essentials of your passport kept separate from your passport.
- Your driver's license if you intend to rent a car.
- At least one pair of long pants, sweatpants, or wind pants.
- Rarely, but some restaurants may require a shirt and slacks, this should be obvious to those of you who may need this.
- #30 suntan lotion – the sun is intense, and you can burn badly in a matter of an hour if your skin has no base.
- Responsible dive or snorkel shops require oil-free or biodegradable (reef safe) sun-block when exploring the reefs, if not, find another guide. It is now Mexican law that you must wear a diving jacket to snorkel near the reefs. This is designed to keep snorkelers from reaching down and touching the coral – enjoy the sights from above or scuba dive.
- Sunglasses, a billed cap, hat or visor.
- Waterproof fanny pack or a small dive pack when in the water (available from Amazon, any international or Mexican dive shop) for valuables, keys, money, etc. Most hotels have a safe for passports, visas, airline tickets, etc.

– The obvious hygiene essentials as they are much more expensive in Mexico, so bring them if you can, just so liquids and gels are 3.4 oz. or less for airline security. Toothpaste, brushes, deodorant, shampoo, suntan lotion, lip gloss, women's hygiene items, band-aids, a small tube of triple antibiotic gel for potential cuts, mosquito repellent (with DEET), the non-aerosol spray kind, a few plastic bags (like freezer bag size at least) to carry things that might open in your luggage and get all over everything.
– A great travel book like "Local Knowledge Travel Guides/Best of Cozumel."
– Drink lots of bottled water, it will compensate for the intense sun and alcohol (if you indulge) which will cause serious dehydration and possible illness, Stay hydrated!
– Tweezers, Ibuprofen, Dramamine (if you are prone to seasickness).
– Phone chargers and headphones
– Be aware of food that has sat out in the hot sun, including lettuce, fruit, or buffets. Restaurants along this coast are highly regulated by the health department, lettuce is generally fine, they can't afford to get people sick, nor do they need that reputation anymore. Food and drink in the local restaurants are safe and excellent in nearly all cases – enjoy them!

INTERESTING FACTS

Coconuts Bar on the east side of Cozumel is the highest point on the island.

Punta Sur (south point) on Isla Mujeres, is the highest point in the Yucatan peninsula.

Sian Ka'an Biosphere Reserve, just south of Tulum, covers 1.3 million acres and spans 120 kilometers from north to south, nearly 1/3 of the Caribbean coast of Mexico. Thick jungle, lagoons, bird-life, marine life, outstanding flat fishing, small Mayan ruins, a handful of small resorts, a couple of tiny villages including the isolated and beautiful village of Punta Allen, and a glimpse of what this entire coastline looked like only 40 years ago.

Mexican federal law prohibits touching, poaching, or disturbing sea turtles in any stage of life, including their nests. Violators will be prosecuted and are subject to fines, penalties and jail time. For further information contact: *(www.ceakumal.org, or www.mexiconservacion.org)*.

The first resort along the coast of what is now referred to as "Riviera Maya," was in Akumal.

Until 1974, Cancun was just a turn in the road. No resorts, one flew into Merida, Cozumel, or Chetumal then.

Hotel Molcas in Playa Del Carmen was the first hotel in town, it was stunning. It has since been dwarfed by Playa Del Carmen, but it remains a legacy to the birth of Playa and has only recently closed.

Punta Sur on Isla Mujeres is the easternmost point in Mexico and the first to see the sunrise.

Tulum was the only Maya city ever built along the coast and the last Maya city built.

Isla Mujeres and Cozumel entertained and provided a consistent infrastructure for visitors long before any place along the mainland coast.

The barrier reef (Mesoamerican Reef) that stretches from Isla Contoy to Nicaragua, including those you see around Isla Mujeres, Cozumel, and Belize, is the second-largest barrier reef in the world only to the Great Barrier Reef of Australia.

Banco Chinchorro, off the coast of Xcalak in extreme southern Mexico near Belize, not only offers outstanding diving, but it is the largest coral atoll in the northern hemisphere.

Just 30 years ago, the shore access snorkeling (5'-10' deep) throughout the area was world-class, most notably Garrafon off Isla Mujeres, Chankanaab off Cozumel and Akumal Bay. Most of these shallow reefs have experienced severe damage from a lack of regulation and understanding of human contact with the coral. In some cases, it is too late and others are in varying stages of protection and regrowth. Respect these extremely valuable resources and follow all posted regulations. Some of what remains is beautiful, but much is beyond help.

One of the most fascinating migrations in the world occurs in great numbers from early May through September off the coast of the northern Yucatan where the Caribbean and Gulf of Mexico meet – that of the Whale Shark. This is not exclusive by any means to this part of the world, but their numbers here are among the largest recorded worldwide.

WATER CONDITIONS AND WARNING FLAGS

Be aware of water and swimming conditions, especially when entering the ocean anywhere on the remote east coast of the island. Recognizing the colored flags indicating safety conditions for swimming on any of the beaches is critical to your safety. Currents and undertows can be dangerous on Cozumel's windward side (east side), and typically you will always see safety flags up at San Martin Beach and Playa Chen Rio. Learn to recognize them.

Green Flag – Ideal Swimming Conditions

Yellow Flag – Caution

Red Flag – Swimming Prohibited/Danger

Black Flag – No Swimming/Dangerous Fauna

HELPFUL SPANISH WORDS AND PHRASES

Give it a go if you don't speak Spanish because an attempt is always appreciated and even a thank you (gracias), or please (por favor), goes a long way. Many of the locals speak excellent English, actually, a lot do, but nonetheless, just like using pesos instead of dollars, you are in Mexico.

Yes/No…..Si/No

Please…..Por Favor

Thank you…..Gracias

You're welcome…..De Nada

Excuse me…..Con permiso

Good morning…..Buenos dias

Good afternoon…..Buenas tardes

Good evening…..Buenas noches

Goodbye…..Adios

Where is…..Donde esta

The bank…..El banco

The bathroom…..El bano

Beer…..Cerveza

One more beer please…..Uno mas cerveza por favor

Another beer please…..Otra vez cerveza por favor

What time is it…..Que hora es

Why…..Que

Open…..Abierto

Closed…..Cerrado

I would like…..Me gustaria

The bill please…..La cuenta por favor

How much is it…..Cuanto cuesta

Money exchange…..Casa de cambio

Ashtray…..Un cenicero

Bread…..El Pan

Menu…..La carta

Pepper…..La pimiento

Salt…..la sal

Eggs…..Huevos

Write it down please…..Escribe por favor

Monday…..Lunes

Tuesday…..Martes

Wednesday…..Miercoles

Thursday…..Jueves

Friday…..Viernes

Saturday…..Sabado

Sunday…..Domingo

January…..Enero

February…..Febrero

March…..Marzo

April…..Abril

May…..Mayo

June…..Junio

July…..Julio

August…..Agosto

September…..Septiembre

October…..Octubre
November…..Noviembre
December…..Diciembre
Do you speak English…..Habla usted Ingles
I don't speak Spanish…..No hablo espanol
I don't understand…..No entiendo
Telephone…..telefono
Market…..Mercado
Waiter…..Senor
Breakfast…..Desayuno
Lunch…..Almuerzo
Dinner…..La cena
Enjoy (a toast)…..Salud
Fish…..Pescado
I am sorry…..Lo siento
My name is…..Me llamo
What is your name…..Como se llama
Where are you from…..de donde es
Can you…..Podria
Appetizer…..Apertivo
Drinks…..Bebidas
Shrimp…..Camaron
Lobster…..Langosta
Meat…..Carne
Octopus…..Pulpo
Conch…..Concha
Shark…..Tiburon
Fork…..Tenedor
Spoon…..Cuchara
Knife…..Cuchillo
Seafood…..Mariscos
Cheese…..Queso
Beans…..Frijoles
Antojitos……Snacks
Soup…..Sopa
Kitchen…..Cocina
Table…..Mesa
Home…..Casa
Chair…..La silla
Caution…..Precaucion
Danger…..Peligro
Safe…..Seguro

Speed bump…..Topes (They are everywhere, so learn to recognize this word and the signs saying "topes"!)

COMMON MENU ITEMS AND WHAT THEY ARE

Ceviche

A dish you will see everywhere consisting of either fish, conch, shrimp, lobster, and other seafood, or a combination thereof, marinated in lemon, lime or other citrus marinades and served in a bowl or plate with fried tortilla chips. Ceviche is fabulous!

Churros

A fried pastry, like a Mexican fritter, often found evenings at street stands, and maybe sprinkled with sugar or served with honey.

Chilaquiles

Common on breakfast menus, they are corn tortillas fried until tender with salsas, then served with cream, avocado, refried beans, shredded chicken, cheeses, or just about anything on top.

Chile Rellenos

A stuffed poblano or other large pepper, cooked with cheeses, meats, spices, and then covered in a batter and fried. There are countless variations.

Huevos Motulenos

Fried eggs on a corn tortilla base with refried beans, cheese, and any number of ingredients like ham, red salsa, diced peppers, tomatoes, or onions.

Cochinita Pibil

A slow cooked pork dish marinated in orange juice, lemon, and or lime, then slow roasted in banana leaves and lathered in achiote paste, a Mexican spice mix. Not easy to find but delicious.

Poc Chuc

A traditional and simple signature Yucatecan dish of pork grilled with a citrus marinade. Most often in the form of a pork chop.

Queso Relleno

A hollowed-out chunk of cheese-filled with pork, spices, maybe chicken, then cooked until the cheese softens. A sloppy and yummy mess!

Salbute

A puffy deep-fried tortilla topped with any number of diced meats, lettuce, avocado, and other options. A popular evening meal.

Sopa De Lima

A staple on menus, Sopa De Lima is a shredded chicken and lime soup with spices, veggies, and often cilantro.

Sopes

With countless variations, it is essentially a piece of fried masa (a ground corn dough) topped with meats, refried beans, cheese, salsas, onions, and many other possibilities.

Flan

A custard-like baked dessert, either egg-based and or with milk or cream, and topped with caramel, honey, vanilla, coconut, and lots of other options.

Molletes

An open-faced thin bread treat topped with cheese, maybe refried beans and salsas.

Huevos Rancheros

A breakfast dish of lightly fried tortillas topped with fried eggs, salsas, refried beans, rice, guacamole, and any other number of ingredients.

Quesadillas

A folded and typically corn tortilla grilled and filled with cheeses, various meats, beans, and nearly any other ingredient and spice.

Empanadas

A corn dough (masa) turnover baked or fried with meats, cheeses, fish, corn, or even as a sweet dessert with cream and fruit fillings.

Tamales

A time consuming traditional Mexican dish made of a corn-based dough, steamed in banana leaves or a corn husk and filled with fruit, or more commonly meats, cheeses, veggies, and other spices and ingredients. The husk is discarded before eating or can be used as an impromptu plate!

Tortas

An open-faced sandwich typically of a flat bread covered in nearly anything.

Huaraches

A fried oblong-shaped masa dough with any number of salsas, potato, onion, tomatoes, meats and topped with melted cheese.

Tix 'n Chic

A traditionally grilled fish recipe with achiote and citruses such as orange juice, lemon and lime, spices, and grilled skin down.

Mole

A mysterious and complicated traditional Mexican paste or powder that can take hours if not days to make. Often chocolate based, but many rich and thick varieties of mole exist. It is a complex blend of ingredients that may be based on something, but only tastes like mole! Unique and nearly different each time you try it.

"Humor is mankind's greatest blessing"

Mark Twain

ABOUT THE AUTHOR

The author has been traveling to the area for over 40 years and has seen it grow from a quiet haven for backpackers and the adventurous diver to its current status as one of the world's premier scuba destinations and cruise ship ports. His passion for Cozumel, as well as the hospitality of the local people, will translate into a more comfortable and insightful vacation for the readers of this book.

It was early evening 1976 and dusk was settling in. The miles of empty sand belonged to nobody but the two of us. We had walked from the cracked and narrow highway 307 to these (Playa Del Carmen) beaches that held not a soul but Jeffrey and me. The few fishermen had already folded up their nets and gone home. That evening, camped out by the same ferry pier still in use today, we waited for any sign of the ferry on the horizon but it never came. We were both 19 and our greatest and only concerns then were that we had no beer and there were no girls; we had nothing but a tent, a can of beans, and some fish donated by a local fisherman. We cherished the opportunity to be camped in such a remote and mystical place at the time, but our goal this trip was to visit and explore the island of Cozumel. The blazing driftwood fire and flickering stars, as well as the few distant lights of Cozumel far across the water that night, were all you could see from inside the darkness that surrounded us.

That mystical silent night passed into the morning. When we awoke anxiously searching for any sight of the ferry that was to take us to the island. As we drank what little water we had left and folded up our things into our packs in anticipation of the ferry, fishermen began to arrive again, as well as families loaded with boxes and wrapped up belongings, ready to travel. There were no posted schedules for the ferry, no one to whom you could ask questions, and our only indication was the gathering group of locals. From when we first saw the boat, it seemed an endless hour until it finally arrived at the old wooden pier. Out of nowhere men appeared to help secure the ferry. Tattered ropes a foot in circumference held the boat to the dock, and people gathered and began loading boxes and crates, goats, chickens, and little children, who we assumed came along because the whole family needed to be together, work or not.

Nearly two hours later we completed the crossing from the run-down tiny fishing village of Playa Del Carmen to the already evolving but still fledgling dive destination of Cozumel, Mexico. Jacques Cousteau had helped introduce this island to the world in the late '50's, but was by no means alone, and now by the early '70's, infrastructure had been developed, some hotels were built, cabs, restaurants, and bars were coming into their own and an international airport was in full operation. We walked north of the ferry pier 2 miles or so and between 2 hotels; we had little trouble finding a place to camp, somewhat hidden under a grove of palms along the beach. This was our base for a week; nobody bothered our things as we left them each day and explored the island.

Not that I would leave my belongings as I did here 40 years ago, but the people of Cozumel are as welcoming and hospitable today as they were back then. That first visit to this island left an impression on me like it has so many other travelers that have continued to come back time and time again. Cozumel has since built a reputation as one of the world's premier dive destinations, and even with the onslaught of cruise ships, it maintains its island charm, especially if you explore.

Kip

Local Knowledge Travel Guides

(Creating travelers out of tourists!)

LOCAL KNOWLEDGE TRAVEL GUIDES/ BEST OF ISLA MUJERES

Travel books rarely provide the tourist such a clear, succinct, and simple path to a destination as do Jackson (Kip) Lindsay's Local Knowledge Travel Guides. "Creating travelers out of tourists," as Kip says, may just exemplify the essence of what these remarkable guides offer the reader. His 45 years traveling southern Mexico's Yucatan coast, Cozumel and Isla Mujeres, offer a perspective and experience here few have. The books provide the reader with an in-depth opportunity to know places that will fit their style for food and drink, romantic beaches, quiet shopping spots, local music, and art, or top-notch silver your first day, without fumbling around with questionable suggestions. The unique format categorizing dining options, dive and snorkel opportunities, beaches, daytime activities, nightlife, local doctors and pharmacies or shopping venues, enables the visitor to easily select options to their taste immediately upon arrival. For example, Local Knowledge will not just leave you with a list of restaurants, rather it is categorized with "great tacos," ice cream and dessert shops," "choice steaks," "romantic settings for dinner", "beautiful beachside dining", "local seafood", "family dining", "for the vegetarian", etc.

Several media reviews have featured Local Knowledge Travel Guides in the past, including The Denver Post, The Sacramento Bee, and Milwaukee Magazine. In addition, Jackson's writing has been featured on Funjet's Vax Vacation Access, with his stories on Riviera Maya travel destinations, Cancun, Isla Mujeres, and Cozumel.

Jackson's wife Sue has been visiting southern Mexico for a bit longer than he has. Her travels began in the Yucatan, Belize, and Guatemala a couple of years before his, following the "Gringo Trail" like so many young backpackers did in those days. This part of Mexico then was nothing like today. Cancun and Playa Del Carmen had no hotels, there was one road, it was a far different world. Both live in Milwaukee where summers are spent with as much pontoon boat time on the river as is possible.

Jackson (Kip) Lindsay

4113 W. Freistadt Rd.

Mequon, Wi. 53092

Contoy
Holbox
El Cuyo
Isla Mujeres
Cancun
Valladolid
Yucatan
Puerto Morelos
Punta Maroma
Punta Bete
Playa Del Carmen
Puerto Aventuras
Cozumel
Coba'
Xcaret
Kantenah
Xpu-Ha'
Akumel
Xel-Ha'
Riviera Maya
Tulum
Quintana Roo
Boca Paila